# HER MONEY RULES!

## Defining and Achieving Financial Freedom Your Way, From Early Retirement to Investing for Wealth

SHANDA K. MILLER

PINE BENCH

PINE BENCH PUBLISHING
Eugene, Oregon

Published by Pine Bench Publishing, Eugene, Oregon



For more information, email support@pinebenchpublishing.com.

Paperback ISBN: 978-1-7337128-0-4
Hardcover ISBN: 978-1-7337128-6-6
eBook ISBN: 978-1-7337128-1-1
First Edition 2026

## DOWNLOAD THE FREE COMPANION FINANCIAL PLANNER

Thank you for choosing to invest in your financial future by reading this book. For the best experience and to implement the nine money rules faster, download and use the free companion *Her Money Rules! Financial Planner.* As you read and complete each chapter's action plan, use the planner worksheets to build your personal financial plan. Use the planner's implementation worksheets to stay on track, take consistent action, and achieve financial freedom your way.

Get the *Her Money Rules! Financial Planner* at hermoneyrules.com/bonus

*I dedicate this book to my parents, who raised me to be a self-reliant, independent woman. I'm grateful for everything they taught me about money and life. Above all else, I thank them for believing I could do anything and be anyone. It never mattered that I was a girl—all I had to do was dream it, work hard for it, and believe it, too.*

# CONTENTS

# INTRODUCTION

*"If you don't find a way to make money while you sleep, you will work until you die." —Warren Buffett*[1]

The above quote by Warren Buffett, CEO of Berkshire Hathaway Inc., perfectly captures this book's core message and my personal pursuit of financial freedom.

Financial freedom is having enough money to live the life of your dreams without depending on a traditional job. This can also be called financial independence. Both mean having control over your money, time, and life choices. You get to live where you want and spend your time how you want. If you want to travel, you can travel. If you want to volunteer your time on the causes you care about, you can do that.

Financial freedom means you're wealthy and financially secure—you're on *Easy Street.*

Since you've picked up this book, it's possible that you too have a goal of financial freedom, or to build wealth for other reasons. I'm delighted to inform you that this book is your guide to financial freedom—and so much more.

## WHEN CAN I SAVE ENOUGH MONEY SO I CAN QUIT MY JOB AND TRAVEL THE WORLD?

I asked myself this question just a few months into my first job after college. I was twenty-three. It was a year after my first trip to Europe, a trip that sparked my love of travel.

That question—*when can I save enough money so I can quit my job and travel the world?*—began the formation of a goal that would transform over time, even when it seemed unattainable.

After college, I focused on keeping my expenses low. This allowed me to pay off my student loan debt within a year, while I also began investing in my company's 401(k).

When I was twenty-six, I went back to school to get my master's degree. After graduate school, I had a new degree and a new job. But I also had new student loans and credit card debt. I was back to square one with my investing goal after cashing out my investments to get through graduate school. Because of my new student loan and credit card debt, my net worth was negative $40,000.

At thirty-two, my goal was still a pipe dream. I was newly married, had a mortgage, and while my income had increased, so had my living expenses. I realized I wasn't prioritizing saving and investing. My financial actions didn't align with my financial goals.

I realized that if nothing changed, I would be in my sixties before I could quit my job and travel full time. It was going to take me *thirty more years* to realize my dream.

But that's the norm, isn't it? The traditional path for most people is working until they retire, usually in their sixties. But

I didn't want to wait thirty years to reach my dream, and I don't think *you* should have to wait that long either.

I wanted the freedom to spend my days the way I wanted to. Thinking I had another thirty years before I could retire was frustrating; I felt stuck. Maybe you can relate to that feeling. Maybe you're feeling stuck right now.

Fast-forward to my forty-second birthday. I packed up my office and finally left the eight-to-five grind behind. It took me almost twenty years to have the financial means to quit my job and travel the world, but I did it!

So, what changed? What happened in the ten years between the age of thirty-two, when I felt stuck and frustrated, and the age of forty-two?

## Investment Property

When I was thirty-three, I purchased my first investment property, became a landlord, and started a rental business with my husband, Kent.

Two years later, Kent and I bought a second rental property. That's when I realized how powerful rental income could be in helping me reach my financial goals. I realized rental properties were my golden ticket.

Kent also shared my love of travel. My big financial goal became *our* big financial goal.

After buying our second investment property, we created a seven-year plan to reach our goal. The plan included a vision statement for our dream life, as well as short-term goals and action steps. One short-term goal was to pay off my student loans; another was to use part of our income to build an accessory unit on one of our rental properties.

We created a dream board that included our vision statement and short-term goals, along with images that represented our dream life. To make it more personal, we added photos of ourselves in Amsterdam and Paris, along with one of me writing in a coffee shop. We even pasted a magazine cutout of the camper van we hoped to own. Then we hung the board in our bedroom, right next to a world map.

As we pursued our financial goals, my beliefs about money changed. I came to believe that abundance was possible. I realized I could enjoy a good life and feel financially secure now, while still working toward financial freedom in the future.

## Multiple Income Streams

As I watched my financial outlook improve, I realized the power of multiple income streams. Because of the extra income from our rental properties, I saw our path to wealth accelerate. We used this extra income to pay off debt, reinvest in our rental business, and build our savings. This encouraged me to look for additional sources of income.

Besides our two rental properties, we found creative ways to earn more income. For example, Kent and I turned the old garage behind our house into a vacation rental. That same year, I also discovered a new company called Airbnb.

At the height of our income, we were earning from four primary sources: my job, Kent's flooring business, our vacation rental, and two rental properties. I eventually wrote my first book, *From Supervisor to Super Leader*, which also became a source of income.

Soon, we were sitting pretty!

## YOU TOO CAN SOON BE SITTING PRETTY

No matter where you decide to invest—whether in rental properties, the stock market, or a business venture—start as soon as possible. The sooner you invest, the faster you can reach financial freedom.

I acknowledge that the real estate market is vastly different from what it was in my thirties, and the cost of housing has become prohibitively expensive for most. Even so, I still believe there are opportunities to build wealth in both real estate and the stock market, and this book will show you how to find them.

I dedicated this book to my parents for modeling smart money habits. But I wrote this book for you and all women who are ready to take control of their financial lives. You are worthy and capable, and I want you to have access to all the best financial knowledge, all the knowledge I've gained on my journey to financial freedom and fulfillment.

This is the book I wish someone had gifted me twenty years ago.

I believe that all women have the ability and right to be financially independent, financially free, and financially fulfilled. These are your rights, but you must exercise them, and do right by your current and future self. This book will guide your way and help you believe it is possible.

## NINE MONEY RULES FOR FINANCIAL FREEDOM

Whether you're getting started in your twenties, thirties, or beyond, you too can reach your big financial goal in the next ten years.

In this book, I share nine money rules to guide your journey to financial freedom and wealth.

Each chapter focuses on one of these nine money rules:

Rule 1. Transform how you think about money
Rule 2. Get clear on your big financial goal
Rule 3. Cut your biggest expenses first
Rule 4. Create your perfect budget
Rule 5. Grow your income and create multiple income streams
Rule 6. Build your emergency fund
Rule 7. Pay off all your non-mortgage debt
Rule 8. Choose your investment strategy
Rule 9. Implement your financial plan and track your progress

My goal was to write an engaging and easy-to-read book that includes practical steps you can implement right away. This book is a quick read, so it would be easy for you to blow through these nine money rules quickly. But don't skip the action plan steps. If you read the whole book straight through, I highly suggest going back and taking time to re-read each chapter and complete the action plans step by step.

## MONEY STRATEGIES ARE SIMPLE, BUT NOT EASY

Many things in life are simple but not easy, like losing weight. We know losing weight is as simple as eating fewer calories than our body requires, yet implementing weight loss strategies isn't easy. It's the same with saving money. Spending less money than we earn is a simple concept, but it's difficult to implement.

As humans, we often follow our emotions instead of logic. Logically, we know we should build an emergency fund, pay off debt—*and stop adding more*—and invest for the future. It makes sense. It's simple. But that doesn't mean it's easy.

The reason practicing great money habits isn't easy is because our emotions get in our way. We may have also adopted bad habits, which can be hard to break.

As I outlined the topics for this book, I started with the logical strategies and habits I learned on my own financial journey. However, I knew it was important to tackle this aspect of emotional intelligence first.

Thus, the first chapter, Rule 1, focuses on helping you manage your thoughts and attitudes about money.

Then, Rule 2 provides you with the steps to create your big financial goal and inspires a new world of financial possibilities for your life.

After Rules 1 and 2, you'll be ready and pumped to learn specific strategies and habits. Rules 3 through 9 will help you with the how. You'll learn what to do and what not to do on your journey to financial strength and wealth.

## AMELIA'S STORY

Before diving into the nine money rules, I need to share this story with you.

I'll never forget the day my best friend from college, Amelia, told me her marriage had ended. My heartbreak turned to devastation upon learning that wasn't the complete story.

Shortly after graduating from college, Amelia got married, started teaching, and began saving for retirement.

After the birth of their first child, Amelia and her husband decided to move to his hometown to be closer to his parents. Consequently, Amelia cashed out her retirement savings to help fund the move.

Soon after they moved, Amelia and her husband had their second child. A few years later, Amelia returned to teaching and built a stable life. She had a steady job, a healthy family, and a strong, supportive community.

Then seventeen years into her marriage, her husband had an affair with another woman and filed for divorce.

But that wasn't the worst of it. During the untangling of their lives, Amelia found out their finances were a disaster. She had allowed her husband to manage the finances and assumed he was putting a portion of their income into retirement accounts. He lied to her. In truth, she found out they had no savings of any kind.

Because of that, Amelia was now in her early forties, facing the realization that she was on her own, starting from nothing, on a teacher's salary.

## YOU ALONE ARE RESPONSIBLE FOR YOUR FINANCIAL LIFE

As a woman, it's important to understand the value of staying in control of your finances. Regardless of your upbringing or what your current situation is, remember this simple truth: Never hand over control of your money to anyone else.

That doesn't mean you have to take full control of your finances alone or manage everything for both you and your spouse. What I'm suggesting is you equally and jointly control your finances together.

You might choose to keep your finances separate instead. In that case, you and your partner can agree on how to split household and shared expenses. But you'll still keep full control over the rest of your income and investments.

To decide what works best, have open and honest conversations with your spouse. Talk about your financial goals, habits, and whether you're on the same page.

Women have only had full control of their money for about fifty years. Before 1974, most women in the U.S. couldn't open bank accounts or get credit cards without getting a signature from their father, brother, or husband.[2] Since our financial rights are relatively new, it would be foolish not to take full advantage of those rights. We no longer need anyone to approve our financial decisions. We now have full and ultimate control of our financial destiny.

How you choose to live your life and what dreams you choose to pursue are up to you. Why not dream big and create a life you really love?

You don't have to keep living the same life or stay on the same path. Instead, you can start fresh, take an alternative path, and create the life of your dreams. Now is the time to begin your financial journey to freedom. Don't delay reading this book or creating your financial plan.

In reading this book and completing the action plan steps, you'll get:

- A clear and defined financial goal and a detailed plan to reach that goal.

- The right money mindset for being determined and unstoppable in reaching your big financial goal.
- The knowledge and action steps you need to cut expenses and increase your income.
- An investment strategy and plan to speed up your journey to wealth and financial freedom.

Take action today to create a life you love. Use the companion *Her Money Rules! Financial Planner* to complete the action steps at the end of each chapter and build your own financial plan. You can download your free digital copy of the companion planner at hermoneyrules.com/bonus.

Remember, reaching financial freedom isn't easy. It takes hard work, patience, and a change in how you think about money. Stay strong, keep going, and push through challenges to reach your goals faster—your journey starts today!

# RULE 1

# TRANSFORM HOW YOU THINK ABOUT MONEY

*"All that we are is the result of what we have thought." —Buddha*[1]

## CHANGING HOW WE THINK ABOUT MONEY CHANGES OUR ACTIONS

Transforming how you think about money is the first rule for reaching financial freedom.

You want to be determined and unstoppable in taking the actions that lead to reaching your financial goals. Strong financial habits are as important as brushing your teeth. And transforming how you think about money will make building those financial habits a lot easier.

I mentioned in the Introduction that money strategies are simple, but not easy. The reason doing right with our money is hard is because of our deep-rooted money beliefs and bad habits. Our bad habits can include impulse spending, not having a savings cushion, not creating a spending budget, and relying on debt to cover expenses.

Changing how you think about money requires looking into the past and recognizing your money beliefs. You must understand how your beliefs about money developed. Below,

I've provided ten common money beliefs to assist you in identifying your own money beliefs. Once you know your money beliefs, you can choose new beliefs and a new path.

Often, people hold mistaken beliefs about money. To help you choose a new path, I've also included twenty money truths at the end of this chapter. Many people who have built wealth and reached their big financial goals learned these truths along the way. I want you to know and understand these truths.

## AMY'S STORY: HOW MONEY BELIEFS CAN RULE OUR FINANCIAL LIVES

Like me, my friend Amy also owns rental properties and has a big financial goal of reaching financial freedom.

Amy lacked a lot growing up. Her parents struggled to provide basic needs, let alone the things Amy wanted.

As an adult, she was determined to create a life without scarcity. Amy saw what her parents had and hoped she would do something different. Something better.

Amy began reading personal finance books in high school. She also took a career class, where she learned about high-paying jobs in fields like healthcare, engineering, and finance.

With this new knowledge, she realized she could make a good life and earn a lot of money; it was possible to have a career and make a six-figure income. She'd be able to save some of her income and not have to live paycheck to paycheck, as well as have enough money to do meaningful things with it. She saw money as a positive force in her life.

## Scarcity versus Abundance

Amy's parents had a set of beliefs that trapped them in a money scarcity mindset. For example, Amy's mom often said, "I don't even have a dime." This saying reflected how her mom thought about money. Yet Amy was resolute in not wanting to fall into that same mindset. She wanted to let go of scarcity as a way of thinking.

Amy understood you can either have an abundance mindset or a scarcity mindset. A scarcity mindset is when you believe money is limited and people have to compete for their share of the pie. This can lead to feelings of fear and anxiety. In contrast, an abundance mindset is when you believe that resources and opportunities are plentiful and available to all. This mindset can spark generosity and optimism. Amy chose an abundance mindset.

When Amy is worried about money, or wonders if she's making the right decision or not, she'll find a dime on the ground. And finding a dime always makes her step back and remember that everything's going to be okay. Instead of her mom's expression, "I don't even have a dime," Amy's motto is "There are dimes everywhere."

Amy's father had an expression similar to her mother's. He often said, "I'm going to work until the day I die." Amy sees the truth, though. Her dad created his life to be that way. He's an artist and owns a studio. Money isn't his thing.

Amy didn't want to have her dad's mindset either. She doesn't want to work until the day she dies. She knows that with the right mindset and actions, she won't have to. Of course, if she's enjoying meaningful work, she'd be glad to do it for the rest of her life. But she doesn't want to feel like she has to.

Amy's goal is to generate enough passive income, no matter how long it takes, so she doesn't have to think about money again. She wants to have enough for her and her family to live a modest life. She doesn't need enough money for an extravagant life, but enough for a pleasant life. Her goal is financial freedom.

Amy believes being financially free will save her from having to live the life she grew up with. She wants a better life for her family and her children.

She also recognizes that she still has a limiting belief. Once, Amy said, "There will never be enough money in the world to make me feel secure, because I'm running from something that's so deep inside of me."

Thus, Amy admits she still has work to do, changing how she thinks about money. Whenever she catches herself thinking negative thoughts, such as *I'll never feel secure*, she reminds herself she's on the right path. She also repeats positive affirmations, such as:

- *I am safe, supported, and provided for.*
- *I currently have everything I need.*
- *Money flows to me constantly.*

Going from a scarcity mindset to an abundance mindset doesn't happen overnight. Amy is still taking steps toward her big money goals. Yet the closer she gets, the more achievable they feel.

## WHAT WE BELIEVE, WE BECOME

We are what we believe, because we become what we believe is possible. In other words, we limit what is possible in our lives by what we think is possible.

The same holds in our financial lives. If you don't believe you'll become wealthy or achieve financial freedom, you probably won't.

We're not always aware of the beliefs we hold deep down. But those beliefs shape how we think, and our thoughts lead to emotions. Our emotions then influence the decisions we make and the habits we form. Over time, the results of those decisions can reinforce our original beliefs.

That's why your beliefs about money play such a big role in your financial life. They shape your money habits and create your financial reality. Sometimes, these beliefs can even harm your financial health. If you're having a hard time with money, take a deeper look, because your money beliefs might be part of the problem.

## TEN COMMON MONEY BELIEFS

Below are ten common money beliefs. I have not listed these beliefs in any order. They are examples intended to help you reflect on your own unique beliefs about money.

Everyone has different beliefs about money. Sometimes, those beliefs can even contradict each other. For instance, you might believe that money is bad, yet also think that having more of it would solve your problems.

Once you recognize your money beliefs, you can question them, break any bad financial habits, and improve your overall financial health.

### 1. I'm Terrible with Money

If you are someone who believes you're terrible with money, then your behavior and habits may ensure this belief comes true.

If you believe you're terrible with money and you feel anxious when you think about money, you might avoid opening your bills. Thus, you may not pay them on time. Then, late fees and interest may accrue, reinforcing your belief that you're terrible with money.

Similarly, you risk staying or becoming poor if you believe, because your family is poor, you'll be poor too.

Someone who believes they're terrible with money might also have these related thoughts:

- *This job is the best I'll ever have.*
- *I'll never be able to stop living paycheck to paycheck.*
- *Living in a comfortable home or driving a nice reliable car is something I'll never be able to afford.*
- *I'll never get out of debt.*

### 2. Money Equals Success

If you believe that more money means more success—and being seen as successful matters to you—you're more likely to become a top earner.

If you believe money equals success, then you probably feel happy when you buy new things, like electronics, accessories, and clothes. You might go shopping a lot, and risk spending more than you earn.

Likewise, if you believe money equals success, your self-worth may be based on how much money you have or earn. Thus, if you experience a financial setback, such as losing your job, you might face emotional struggles.

As someone who believes money equals success, you might also have these related thoughts:

- *If I invest in an education or a skill, it'll help me be successful and land a good job.*
- *I'm great at what I do, so I'm going to go after that promotion.*
- *Because I know I can always earn more money, I don't have to worry about spending too much or going into debt.*
- *I deserve to drive a fancy car and own the latest iPhone.*

### 3. Money Buys Happiness

If you are someone who believes having more money leads to more happiness, well...you're like most people!

Research shows that money can contribute to happiness. Money helps people meet their basic needs, reduce financial stress, and create more opportunities. But this belief can be tricky. Money is only one part of happiness, and its impact only goes so far.

Also, you may believe that having more money will help solve your problems. This can also be true, but again, only to a certain degree.

If you believe money buys happiness, you might enjoy spending it on shiny new things. But that happiness often fades once the novelty wears off, and you might repeat the cycle when another shiny object catches your eye.

You might also enjoy spending money on others because you wish to make them happy. If you spend money to increase your or others' happiness, you risk spending more than you earn. Thus, you risk setting yourself up for high debt and financial strain.

Related thoughts you might have with the belief that money buys happiness:

- *If I just buy this thing, then I'll feel happier.*
- *I deserve to spend my money on things that make me feel good.*
- *This latest new smartphone will be fun and make my life easier.*
- *It feels good to buy things for my daughter because I want her to be happy.*
- *I earned my raise. So I deserve to reward myself with a new wardrobe.*

### 4. Money is Hard to Get

If you believe money is scarce, you might reinforce this belief by overlooking opportunities to earn more. You might not invest your money because you fear the risk of losing it.

You might not invest in increasing your skills, education, or personal growth because you need to save every penny.

The belief that money is hard to get is a scarcity belief. You might also believe that there will never be enough money. So why bother trying harder to get more?

The belief that money is hard to get may stem from a belief in your inability to earn more. You may also underestimate your skills and abilities.

As someone who believes money is hard to get, you might also have these related thoughts:

- *I have to work twice as hard as everyone else to make even a little money.*
- *Since money is scarce, I might as well spend this extra money now.*
- *Dreaming about being rich or reaching financial freedom is unrealistic for someone like me.*
- *Rich people are lucky or are born rich.*
- *It's impossible to get ahead in the current economy.*

### 5. There Will Always Be Enough Money

You might be someone who believes there will always be enough money. While having a positive mindset about money is great, a casual attitude about money could be harmful to your long-term financial well-being.

If you believe money will always be there, you may put off saving or investing for the future. You may spend more than you make and accumulate debt. You might underestimate the risk of losing your job or a business investment.

In addition, if you believe money is abundant, you might delay financial planning. Thus, it may be more difficult for you to achieve your long-term financial goals.

As someone who believes there will always be enough money, you might have these related thoughts:

- *Why save money? There will always be more money when I need it.*
- *I'm going to purchase this luxury item because I can afford it now, and I can always save money later.*
- *I'm a top earner, so I don't need to budget my money.*
- *This business looks like a promising investment, but if it doesn't work out, I can always build up my savings again.*

### 6. I Don't Deserve to Have Money

You might believe you don't *deserve* to have money. This belief may arise from deeper issues, such as having low self-worth, guilt, or limiting beliefs. The belief that you don't deserve to have money can affect your ability to build financial stability. You might not see yourself as capable of building or maintaining wealth.

If you believe you don't deserve to have money, you might be frivolous or impulsive with your spending. You probably don't save money or take part in financial or career planning, both of which could improve your financial future. You might also undervalue your skills and abilities and avoid going after better-paying jobs or promotions.

Associated thoughts you might have with the belief that you don't deserve to have money:

- *Someone else needs money more than I do.*
- *I don't deserve to earn more than I already do, because I'm not skilled or educated enough.*
- *No one will pay me more for my services because I'm not worth more.*
- *I'm bad with money, so I don't trust myself with it.*

### 7. Money is Bad

You might be someone who believes that money is bad, full stop. Likewise, you may believe money corrupts and rich people are greedy.

As someone who believes money is bad, you might not want to think about or deal with money. With this belief, you may avoid career growth opportunities. Thus, you probably won't invest in your personal or professional growth.

Believing money is bad may lead to feelings of guilt about earning or keeping money. This could lead to self-sabotaging your financial health. You might avoid building wealth, and you might spend more than you earn or give your money away.

Choosing not to build wealth will make it difficult to achieve financial security. Thus, limiting your ability to create a better or more fulfilling life, or contribute to causes you care about.

If you believe that money is bad, you might also have these thoughts:

- Money is the root of all evil.
- Rich people must have done something unethical to get their wealth.
- People will judge me or think I'm greedy if I have money.
- There is virtue in living with less money.

### 8. Money is Not Important

You may have the belief that money is not important. You might also believe wealth has nothing to do with happiness, status, or self-worth.

While money has a limited effect on happiness, believing it's unimportant may keep you from thinking about or practicing basic financial habits. You may also be lax about earning money, saving money for emergencies, or planning and investing for the future. You may further neglect your financial health by not focusing on career growth.

Without practicing good financial habits, you may struggle to meet basic needs, handle emergencies, or achieve long-term financial goals. You may end up with high debt and no savings, thus setting yourself up for financial difficulties.

While money alone may not buy happiness, it's a tool for providing basic needs, stability, and meaningful opportunities.

If you believe that money is not important, you might also have these thoughts:

- *I don't need to earn much as long as I'm happy.*
- *As long as I have enough for today, I don't need to worry about money.*
- *I don't need a lot of money to be happy or secure, so investing money is unnecessary.*
- *Money is an abstract concept, so debt means nothing to me.*
- *Anytime I need money, the universe provides.*

### 9. Money is Security

You may believe money is security, and perhaps this belief has made you somewhat obsessed with earning or saving money.

Money plays a role in providing stability. Yet putting too much focus on it can have unintended consequences. You might risk burnout, stress, or other health issues if you prioritize long work hours in pursuit of financial security. Not spending enough on basic needs could also affect your health, personal happiness, or relationships.

With an overemphasis on viewing money as security, you may overlook other aspects of having a secure life. Such as mental resilience, healthy relationships, and personal freedom.

If you believe that money is security, you might also have these thoughts:

- *I have to keep earning more money to feel secure.*
- *The more money I have, the more secure I'll be.*
- *If I spend money, I'll risk not having enough for my safety net.*
- *Even though I have a lot of money saved, I still feel anxious that I don't have enough.*

### 10. Money Gives My Life Meaning

You may believe that money gives your life meaning. But while money can facilitate our pursuit of creativity, personal connections, and purpose, it alone can't create true fulfillment.

If you tie your sense of purpose too closely to money, you may constantly chase more. You may never feel satisfied, no matter how much you earn or save. This can lead to a persistent sense of discontent.

This belief might also lead you to stay in a high-paying job you dislike, sacrificing passion and purpose for a paycheck. Even with financial success, you may feel unfulfilled. In pursuing wealth, you might overlook your health, relationships, or personal growth—all of which are essential to lasting happiness and meaning in life.

If you believe that money gives your life meaning, you might also have these thoughts:

- *Growing my wealth is my ticket to a meaningful and enjoyable life.*
- *My life will lose meaning if I stop working.*
- *I'll be happy once I reach a specific financial milestone.*

## Emotional Decisions versus Objective Decisions

Which of the ten common money beliefs resonate with you? How do you think these beliefs affect your decisions regarding money?

Most of us are not aware of how much our thinking and beliefs drive our emotions, nor how much our emotions drive our decisions. Unfortunately, we make our worst decisions with our emotions.

Instead, we need to think through our money decisions objectively.

Recognizing that our beliefs and emotions shaped our past decisions gives us the chance to make more intentional, thoughtful decisions about money today.

We can also practice being aware of our emotions, learn to ride them out, and give them time and space. We can then redirect our attention back to our financial goals and our financial plan. By making money decisions and taking action based on our goals and plans, we can reach our big financial goals more logically and effectively.

## TWENTY MONEY TRUTHS

Now that you've learned some common money beliefs and related thoughts, I'd like to switch focus and share some common money truths.

Money truths are logical money realities, as identified by financial experts or experienced by people who have reached financial wealth.

1. We measure rich people by their income. The rich usually have a lot of cash to spend on goods and services. Yet not all rich people are wealthy. Some rich people are big spenders and appear wealthy, but they spend more than they invest.
2. Unlike rich people, we measure wealthy people by their net worth. Net worth is not a measure of income. Instead, net worth is the total value of cash, investments, and assets you own, minus how much you owe in debt. In truth, most wealthy people are not big spenders, and you may not even realize they are wealthy based on external clues.
3. Money is a tool meant to help you meet basic needs, experience life, have more freedom, or fulfill a dream. You can also use money as a tool for earning more money, such as by investing in your personal growth and development.
4. If you always spend more than you earn, you'll eventually face financial ruin. If you want to become wealthy, you'll need to spend less than you earn, and invest the rest.

5. Most millionaires are not born into wealth, nor are they lottery winners. In fact, 79 percent of millionaires are self-made, according to a Ramsey Solutions study. Most of these self-made millionaires reached that milestone by investing every month over a long period. Most self-made millionaires did not earn high salaries. They were normal people with normal jobs.[2]
6. In the long-term, spending money on items you don't need will not make you happier. Actually, studies have found that materialism is negatively associated with life satisfaction.[3] Instead, research shows that investing in life experiences, such as travel, recreation, and restaurant meals, is more likely to bring people happiness than material things.[4]
7. Wealthy people do whatever it takes to build wealth. They budget and track their spending every month. They live on less than they earn. The wealthy sacrifice early on. They understood, the sooner they sacrificed by investing a large portion of their income, the sooner they'd become wealthy. The wealthy prioritize investing for the future, ahead of meeting today's wants and desires.
8. Earning more income alone will not help you build wealth, especially if you continue to spend more than you earn or under-invest. Also, longer hours or a higher-paying job will not solve the problem of spending more than you make.
9. Everything you own and use, such as luxury items, recreational vehicles, cars, and homes, are liabilities, not assets. These are liabilities because they lose value over time or they cost money to maintain or insure. Yet owning investment homes or other items as part

of a business are assets. They are assets because they earn you a return, such as from rents or other profits.[5]

10. Generally, you'll be better off financially in the long term by renting versus owning the home you live in. This is because owning the home you live in is a liability. I further explain the pros and cons of renting versus owning your home in Rule 7.
11. Historically, the value of the U.S. stock market has always gone up. There may be daily, monthly, or annual drops, but over the long-term, the value will continue to climb upward.[6] Similarly, most real estate investments grow in value over time.
12. Most wealthy people took years or decades to build wealth. They did this by routinely investing a portion of their income every month. For example, Warren Buffett gained 99 percent of his wealth after age fifty.[7] Wealthy people understand that get-rich-quick schemes are indeed schemes or scams. If it sounds too good to be true, it is. Don't get scammed. And don't play the lottery for reasons other than entertainment.
13. Wealthy people place more value on time than money. They understand that time is a limited resource. The average number of weeks in an average person's life is four thousand. This shows that we have only a limited amount of time to be alive and experience life. Thus, wealthy people see money as a tool to create more time and freedom. They understand that the sooner they invest, the sooner they can make the most of their time, and eventually stop trading their time for money.

14. Passive income is money earned regularly from a source other than employment or self-employment. Sources of passive income can include rental properties, royalties, dividends, and other investments.
15. You've only reached financial freedom when you've reached the crossover point. The crossover point is when your monthly passive investment income matches your living expenses. The speed at which you reach your crossover point depends on two things: first, how low you can reduce your monthly living expenses; second, how much you can increase your monthly investment profits or other passive income.[8]
16. Investment money compounds, and so does debt. Investment compounding is when your investment money earns money, and that new money then makes more money. Compounding grows exponentially like a snowball, which means your money grows faster and faster and ultimately multiplies. When your money makes money and you invest additional money each month, your investment will compound at an even greater rate. Similarly, debt will compound if you don't pay it off right away.
17. If you keep your money in a savings account or certificate of deposit instead of investing it, your money may lose value because of inflation.
18. Paying off your credit card each month is a requirement for financial health. If you can't pay it in full each month, cut it up. Credit card debt is a sign that you're spending more than you earn.

19. To speed up your path to wealth, you'll need to invest more of your income and make bigger sacrifices. Some common sacrifices include riding your bike or taking the bus, getting a roommate, and packing your lunch.
20. If you're making great sacrifices to reduce your living expenses and you still can't afford to invest, then get a side hustle. A side hustle is a side job, gig, or business you do in your free time to earn extra income.

If you make these twenty money truths your own and take action based on them, you'll become great with money. These truths will also help you reach your big financial goals and build a strong financial life.

In the next chapter, you get to decide on your big financial goal. Once you have your goal, it'll be time to take action.

Goal + Action = Result

Even in the face of your money beliefs and habits, I'm going to ask you to prioritize action. Action over story. Action over worry, and action over self-doubt. Action, because your success with money and reaching your big financial goal depends on it.

## KEY POINTS

- Gaining money skills and implementing money strategies are simple, but not easy.
- We limit what is possible in our lives by what we think is possible.
- Our money beliefs can either get in our way, or they can help us on our path to wealth and financial freedom.
- We make our worst decisions with our emotions. Instead, if we make money decisions and actions based on our goals and plans, we can logically and more effectively reach our goals.
- There are common money truths, and the sooner you understand them, the less likely you are to go down the wrong financial path.

## ACTION PLAN

In the companion *Her Money Rules! Financial Planner*, or your notebook or journal, complete the following action steps:

- [ ] What are your money beliefs and stories? What do you tell yourself about money? Set a timer for five minutes and journal your thoughts.
- [ ] What emotions come up when you have to think about or deal with money? List at least five emotions (e.g., anxiety, joy, frustration, optimism, dread, empowerment, pride, overwhelm). Write about why you feel the way you do about money.

- ▢ Now that you've shed some light on your money beliefs, what is now possible for you? If you could choose now, who would you be? What new money beliefs and money habits can you adopt? Set a timer for five minutes and journal your thoughts.

## COMING UP IN RULE 2: GET CLEAR ON YOUR BIG FINANCIAL GOAL

In the next chapter, you'll learn three steps for reaching any big goal: 1) getting clear on what you really want; 2) believing achieving your goal is possible; and 3) creating and implementing a detailed plan of action. You'll also practice visualizing your life after having accomplished your big financial goal, because if you can see yourself in the future, you're more likely to take action now to reach that future goal.

# RULE 2

# GET CLEAR ON YOUR BIG FINANCIAL GOAL

*"Tell me, what is it you plan to do with your one wild and precious life?"*

*—Mary Oliver*[1]

## PETER'S STORY

Known as Mr. Money Mustache from his financial freedom blog with the same name, Peter Adeney's big financial goal was to "retire from real work" so he could "devote his best hours to being a dad." Raising his son was his biggest priority, and he wanted to dedicate more time to being a dad than a forty-hour workweek allowed.[2]

I call attention to Peter's goal because it includes his *why*—his purpose and reason for wanting to retire early from *real work*.

Peter reached this goal after nine years of working in the tech industry. He reached financial independence at thirty, just in time for his son to be born.[3]

To work toward this big money goal, Peter and his wife invested over 50 percent of their salaries. According to Peter, they could've spent their extra disposable income on "auto loans, higher mortgages, newer clothes and more nights out at the restaurants." He said, "Instead, we spent the money on the ultimate luxury—quitting our jobs."[4]

Rule 2 is all about creating your big financial goal and includes identifying your why.

## THREE STEPS TO REACHING ANY BIG FINANCIAL GOAL

There are three critical steps to reaching any big goal, and I explore each step in more detail below:

- Step 1 is to dream big, find your why, and name your big goal. You want to understand why it's important for you to reach this goal. The more your why comes from your heart's desire, the greater the chance you will reach your goal.
- Step 2 is to believe your big goal is possible for you and includes visualizing what it will be like once you've reached that goal.
- Step 3 is creating a detailed plan for how you'll reach your goal and executing that plan with committed action.

If you haven't already, now is the time to download your free digital copy of the companion *Her Money Rules! Financial Planner.* This planner will guide you through the action steps in this chapter and the ones that follow. It will also help you complete your One-Page Financial Plan, found at the beginning of the planner. If you prefer, you can use a journal or notebook to complete the action steps. No matter how you complete them, following the action steps increases your chances of achieving your financial goals.

## STEP 1: DREAM BIG AND FIND YOUR WHY

### Reflect on Your Desires

The first step in realizing any goal is to get clear on what that goal is. What is your heart telling you? Give yourself permission to dream big. As you're dreaming, set aside any doubts or negative thoughts. Instead, imagine that what you desire is possible. There are no obstacles, and you won't fail in achieving what you want.

Keep in mind, this is about you and your life. What is it you desire versus what you think society or others expect you should have or want? What do you value in life?

Another exercise that may help you dream big is to visualize your perfect day. You can do this either with a journal or by closing your eyes and meditating. Either approach allows you to think about and explore the questions to gain a deeper understanding of your thoughts, feelings, and desires. As you journal or meditate, ask yourself and spend at least three minutes thinking about and exploring each of these questions:

- What does your perfect day look like?
- What do you want to do and experience?
- Where do you want to be?
- What do you want to have and enjoy?

As you explore and think about each question, imagine that nothing will get in your way of reaching what you desire. Set aside any judgement, including ideas of right or wrong. Hold nothing back. Allow yourself to imagine and dream.

Use these additional journal questions to help you connect with what you truly want in life:

- What are ten things you want to *have* before you die? Consider both material and non-material things.
- What are ten things you want to *do* before you die?
- What have you already enjoyed or experienced that you want more of?
- Where do you want to live? Think about both the space you live in and the geographic location.
- Who do you want to spend your days with?

Again, spend at least three minutes journaling or meditating on each of these questions. Once you've gained clarity on your desires, write goals that will help you fulfill those desires. What are some goals that can help turn those desires into reality? Then turn those goals into financial goals. How might money or wealth help you achieve your ideal life?

### Write Down Your Goal

After you've spent a good amount of time thinking about and exploring your desires, identify what you want the *most*. Then turn that into a financial goal—your big financial goal.

Write your big financial goal down. Research studies have consistently shown that people are more likely to achieve their goals if they write them down. A study by psychology professor Dr. Gail Matthews at Dominican University revealed that people who wrote down their goals were 42 percent more likely to achieve them than those who simply thought about their goals.[5]

Next, assign a dollar amount to your goal. This amount may change as you finish reading this book and fill out your financial plan. But for now, provide your best guess of how much you will need to reach your big financial goal.

If your goal is to purchase your dream home, then you'd want to either save up for the down payment or the full price. Assuming the median sale-price of homes is $400,000, then you'd want to save at least $80,000 for a 20 percent down payment.[6]

However, if your goal is to become wealthy or achieve financial freedom, then your investment goal will be a lot higher. To start, you could take Charlie Munger's advice and "find a way to get your hands on $100,000."[7] Munger was a partner of Warren Buffett and the vice chair of Berkshire Hathaway. He believed that reaching your first $100,000 was critical to starting on the path to wealth. Over time, with compound interest and investment opportunities, that amount can grow exponentially.

After writing down your big financial goal as a dollar amount, set a date to achieve it. Maybe it's six months or a year from now, or five or ten years from now. Regardless, you want your *by when* date to be realistic, but also close enough to give yourself some urgency to take action.

If your goal is to save up $80,000 for a down payment on a home, then you could pick your *by when* date to be five to seven years in the future. It may take you less time, but choose a date that feels realistic. Base it on your income and how much you plan to save and invest each month. You can use an online investment calculator to estimate how long it will take to reach your savings goal. One option is the calculator available at calculator.net.

## What is Your Why?

Once you have your goal defined, it's important to get clear on your why. Why do you want to achieve this goal? Why is this goal important to you? How does this goal fit with your values?

If your goal is retiring early or being financially free, ask yourself why you want that. What will it give you? What do you want to do with your time?

No matter what your goal might be, ask yourself what achieving that goal will give you. Then, whatever your response is, ask yourself what that will give you. Ask the question at least three times.

Here's an example of how I determined my why for my financial freedom goal:

> What will financial freedom give you?
> *Answer: It will give me the ability to use my time freely.*

> What will that freedom give you?
> *Answer: The freedom to do what I want with my time, the freedom to spend my time on things I'm passionate about. The ability to pursue my passions, to travel, and to spend more time with my loved ones.*

> What will spending time on things you're passionate about give you?
> *Answer: It will give me fulfillment, joy, and happiness.*

Based on the above example, the goal is to achieve financial freedom. The why is so I can pursue my passions in life, and live a fulfilling, joyful, and happy life.

This exercise will help you get to the heart of what you truly want and why. Understanding your why will help move you toward living the life you want to live.

## STEP 2: BELIEVE IN YOUR DREAM

The second step is to believe you'll be able to reach your big financial goal and fulfill your dream. If you don't believe you'll achieve it, then you probably won't.

To believe you can reach your big financial goal or any big goal, you need to see yourself in the future. This may sound like a simple thing. But if you can't visualize yourself as older and living your life in some future time, you probably won't take actions now toward your future goals.

I talked about beliefs in Rule 1 and how we limit what is possible in our lives by what we think is possible. However, we can change our beliefs and mental models.

Mental models are like beliefs. We form them from our experiences. They give us a framework for how we understand and interact with the world. The theory of mental models is that once we form a belief about something or about ourselves, it takes a lot to change our beliefs. However, one way you can change your mental models and beliefs is to practice visualization.

Every day, take a few moments to visualize that you have already reached your goal. I want you to see and feel what it's like to have your dream as your reality.

Mike Dooley, creator of the daily email *Notes from the Universe*, believes visualization is the most powerful tool for turning your dreams into reality. He suggests spending just five minutes a day visualizing your dream life—as if it's already happening. Use all your senses to fully experience the scene. See it, hear it, feel it. Most importantly, let yourself feel the joy and excitement of living that life. Immerse yourself in the emotion of it.[8]

Try this visualization exercise. I've listed four questions below. Close your eyes and visualize your response. Spend a minute on each question, or four minutes total.

### Visualization Questions:

- What is it like to have reached your big financial goal?
- What feelings are you experiencing?
- Who is there with you to celebrate your accomplishment?
- What are you doing, and what are you experiencing?

Once you've created a vision for your future life, the next step is to embody it in the present. Begin by asking yourself: Who am I being, and who do I need to become to reach my goal? You can choose to be that person starting today. To take it even further, commit fully to becoming the person you need to be to achieve what you desire.

Below is a non-financial example.

### Example: Being a Fit and Healthy Person

In my twenties and thirties, I struggled with my weight. So I created a big goal for myself to reach and maintain a specific weight I determined to be healthy.

During my journey of losing weight and improving my health, I realized the concept of *being* might be the thing I was missing. I refer to *being* here as who I am and how I show up in the world. Am I being someone who is fit and healthy? A better question might be: Am I a fit and healthy person?

I remember thinking about the people in my life whom I considered to be fit and healthy. I asked myself, *What if it is a mindset thing? What if I could think of myself as a fit and healthy person? And better yet, what if I committed to being someone who is fit and healthy now?*

Thus, I began to *be* a fit and healthy person who *did* the things a fit and healthy person would do. I shifted to a mostly whole foods plant-based diet full of fiber and protein. I walked, ran, or biked five days a week, and I also started strength training.

Thinking of myself as a fit and healthy person helped. Committing myself to being that person made taking those actions much easier. Building these habits was easier because there was no longer a question of doing them or not. I did them because I committed to being a fit and healthy person—someone who does fit and healthy things.

### Who Are You Committed to Being?

Let's get back to your big financial goal. Who are you committed to *being now* to achieve that goal?

To help you answer this question, put yourself in the future again. I've listed a few more questions for you to answer below.

Again, either write in your journal or close your eyes and think through what each question is asking you:

- Imagine you have reached your goal. Who have you become to reach that goal?
- Visualize yourself as having become that person. What does it feel like to be that person?
- Choose to be that person right now. What's it like to believe yourself to be that person today?

Commit yourself to being that person now. Committing to becoming the person you need to be to achieve your goal means constantly showing up as that person.

In this step, you've done the visualization exercises to help you believe your dream is possible, and you can now see yourself vividly living that dream. You've also committed to being who you need to be to achieve your goal.

The next step is to take committed action to achieve your goal, as outlined below in Step 3.

## STEP 3: PLAN AND TAKE ACTION TO REACH YOUR DREAM

In the first two steps, you got clear on your big financial goal. You visualized yourself in the future having reached that goal and now believe your goal is possible. Then you committed to being the person you need to be to reach that goal. The third step is to do whatever it takes to achieve that goal. And that includes making a plan.

To create your plan, start by identifying what you need to do to reach your big financial goal. As Tony Robbins said,

"Success leaves clues."[9] If your goal is financial freedom, then find out what other financially free people did to reach that goal themselves.

For instance, I introduced you to Peter earlier in this chapter. He had a goal of retiring early from *real work*. What Peter and his wife did was invest over 50 percent of their salaries in rental properties and the stock market until they reached their goal. They invested their money not on luxury items, but on quitting their jobs.[10]

Rules 3 through 9 in this book also provide examples and plenty of guidance on what to do and how to do it. First, learn what to do. Then create your financial plan, which includes setting smaller goals and action steps to reach your big financial goal.

### Create Your Financial Plan

Once you've learned the different things needed to reach your big financial goal, you can complete your personal financial plan. Your plan should include smaller goals and action items that will move you incrementally toward reaching your big goal.

Besides the what and how, the remaining chapters include strategies and tips you can use to help create your individualized financial plan. When you've finished all the action plan steps, you'll have your One-Page Financial Plan.

### Implement Your Financial Plan

Once you have your One-Page Financial Plan filled out, immediately put it into action.

Put yourself on the path to reaching your big financial goal by implementing the first steps of your plan right away. Don't create a plan and forget about it. Consistent action on your plan is as important as the plan itself.

Also, regularly review your big financial goal and your financial plan, and create a system for tracking your progress.

You want your big financial goal to become your dominating obsession until you reach that goal. Keep taking action on your plan. Do not quit. When things get hard or you have a setback, don't give up. Don't give up when you make a mistake. Instead, learn from that mistake, revise your plan, and keep taking action.

## Grit and Persistence

Once I committed to my seven-year financial plan, I continued to move forward on my big financial goal. I made a lot of mistakes along the way, but I kept taking consistent action. I had the mindset of being unstoppable.

One example of how unstoppable I was is when I set a goal to be promoted to a leadership position in my field. This promotion was a key step in my plan to boost my income, position myself for future opportunities, and become a top earner. I also loved leading people.

Yet when I first applied and interviewed for a leadership position, I didn't get the promotion. A year later, I tried again, but still didn't get the promotion. Yet I was determined, and I continued to improve my skills and ask for more responsibilities.

Finally, management saw that I was ready and promoted me to team leader. Even though it took me longer than I expected to reach that goal, I would not give up. I was unstoppable. I would not quit trying until I became a team leader.

You too must have this mindset of being unstoppable to achieve your big goals. Get clear on what you want and go after it. Take action every day, even if you don't want to or think you can. Honor yourself and your future self by taking persistent action toward reaching your big goal.

To recap, the three steps to reaching any big goal are to:

1. Formulate your dream or goal.
2. Starting now, be the person you need to be to reach your goal and believe that you can reach your goal.
3. Make a plan, and do everything you need to do to reach your goal, and be persistent.

## SMART GOALS

Achieving your big financial goal may seem daunting right now, but if you break it down into smaller goals, it won't feel so out of reach. For your smaller goals, I recommend you create SMART goals.

**S**–Specific: the desired accomplishment is detailed and clear.

**M**–Measurable: the desired accomplishment is quantifiable; you'll know when you've achieved it.

**A**–Achievable: the goal is realistic; it's challenging but manageable.

**R**–Relevant: the goal is connected to and a stepping stone for reaching a bigger goal.

**T**–Time-bound: the goal has a due date; the timeline is ambitious to motivate action.[11]

First, to identify your smaller goals, ask yourself: What will I need to accomplish between now and my end goal? Once you've identified the smaller accomplishments, you can turn those into smaller SMART goals.

Let's use my big goal of financial freedom as an example. My seven-year plan included reaching the following smaller goals:

- Continue to develop professionally in my field and increase my income by becoming a Certified Internal Auditor and earning a leadership promotion at work.
- Increase my rental income by purchasing and renovating a second investment property.
- Build up additional savings and stock investments.

For each of the above goals, I had other smaller goals and turned these into SMART goals as defined above.

### Katie's Non-SMART Goal Example:

*I want to save more money.*

There is nothing specific or measurable about Katie's goal, and it is not clear how or when she'll achieve it.

### Ann's SMART Goal Example:

*I want to save an additional $500 each month to help meet my home down payment goal of $80,000 by 2030.*

Ann's goal is specific and measurable, and it has a due date. Let's assume the goal is also achievable based on her income and spending needs.

However, this down payment savings SMART goal is also pretty big and long term, so Ann broke it up into smaller goals.

Ann knew that to achieve this goal, she needed to make some changes to her spending habits. Thus, she created a smaller, related goal of creating a monthly budget before the first of the next month. She would include a category for Home Savings in her budget and assign $500 per month to this savings category.

Ann also included a smaller goal of downloading the You Need A Budget app to her phone and computer by the following weekend. She plans to use this app to create and track her budget. She also created a goal of entering her spending into the budget app every day, and of reviewing her budget at least once a week.

Once Ann broke her big down payment goal into smaller SMART goals, everything felt more manageable. She shared with me that the process was encouraging. She was excited about implementing her budget and savings plan.

### Your Turn

Practice creating a SMART goal by filling out the SMART Goal Worksheet for one of your financial goals. Pick a goal that is a stepping stone to reaching one of your larger goals.

There are SMART goal worksheets in the companion *Her Money Rules! Financial Planner* or you can download the worksheet at hermoneyrules.com/bonus.

Once you're clear on your big financial goal and the specific milestones to reach it, you can begin turning your smaller goals into SMART goals. To get started, pick one milestone and determine what you need to do this month to help you move closer to that achievement. Then ask yourself: What do I need to do this week? What do I need to do tomorrow?

## KEY POINTS

- There are three steps to reaching any big goal: 1) Dream big, find your why, and name your big goal; 2) Believe your big goal is possible for you; and 3) Create a detailed plan and execute that plan with committed action.
- To achieve your big financial goal, it's important to believe strongly that you can achieve it.
- Clearly imagining your future self after reaching your big financial goal makes it easier to take action now.
- For your big financial goal and smaller milestone goals, use the SMART goal formula to ensure your goals are specific, measurable, achievable, realistic, and time bound.

## ACTION PLAN

In the companion *Her Money Rules! Financial Planner*, or your notebook or journal, complete the following action steps:

- ☐ Related to money and lifestyle, write everything your heart desires. If anything were possible and you knew you would not fail, what is it you would want? Set a timer for ten minutes and journal your thoughts.
- ☐ Write out what your perfect day would look like. What do you want to do and experience? What do you want to have and enjoy? Where do you want to be? Set a timer for ten minutes and journal your thoughts.
- ☐ As you gain clarity about what you want during your one precious life, consider how you can help make that dream life a reality. How might money, wealth, assets, or time help you achieve that ideal life? Set a timer for five minutes and write your thoughts.
- ☐ Formulate your big financial goal. If making your dream life a reality will take money, wealth, or assets, consider how much you will need. Express this goal as a specific dollar amount. Then choose a date by which you will reach your goal. You want your date to be realistic, but also close enough to give yourself some urgency to take action (e.g., By June 2027, I will have achieved my goal of saving up $80,000 for the down payment on my dream home). Record this goal at the top of your One-Page Financial Plan found in the *Her Money Rules! Financial Planner*.
- ☐ Get clear on your why. Why do you want to achieve this goal? Why is this goal important to you? What will you get from accomplishing this goal? Set a timer

for five minutes and journal your thoughts, then write your ultimate why statement (e.g., I want to reach one million net worth so I can pursue my passions, travel, and spend more time with my loved ones).

- ☐ Visualization exercise: Visualize what it'll be like once you've achieved your big financial goal. What feelings are you experiencing? Who is there with you to celebrate your accomplishment? What are you doing, and what are you experiencing? Set a timer for five minutes and meditate on your answers or write your thoughts.
- ☐ You have identified your big financial goal as a number. Now it's time to identify smaller goals. Work backward from your target date to map out smaller milestones you'll need to hit along the way. Write out at least five milestone goals. Then, turn each of your smaller milestone goals into SMART goals. You can download the SMART Goal Worksheet at hermoneyrules.com/bonus. Then include your first four SMART goals on your One-Page Financial Plan.

## COMING UP IN RULE 3: CUT YOUR BIGGEST EXPENSES FIRST

When our living expenses are less than we earn, we can save a portion of our income and build wealth. In the next chapter, you'll learn how you can cut your living expenses by cutting your largest expenses, like housing, transportation, and food. You'll also learn many other expense-cutting options.

# RULE 3

# CUT YOUR BIGGEST EXPENSES FIRST

*"She who buys what she does not need, steals from herself."*
*—adapted from a Swedish proverb*[1]

## LATTES VS. LUXURIES

Your financial mind is in the right place, and you've identified your big financial goal. Now, it's time to make a plan for achieving that goal.

The first part of the plan is to cut expenses and live on less money than you earn. Only then can you build up an emergency fund to help you save even more, start investing, and begin building wealth.

When cutting expenses, most people start by looking at the small expenses that add up during the month. Like cutting out their daily lattes. Many financial experts endorse this method of expense cutting.[2]

Instead, to reduce your living costs drastically, I believe you should start by reducing your largest expenses. Thus, I recommend cutting luxuries before lattes.

## YOUR BIGGEST EXPENSE—HOUSING

One such luxury, and possibly your biggest expense, could be the home you live in.

If you only cut the small expenses like those daily coffee drinks versus brewing at home, you'd be cutting about $100 each month. However, you could save as much as $500, $1,000, or more on housing costs.

How much you can save on housing depends on your current housing situation and how much flexibility you have. Are you renting or buying? Are you single or married? Do you have children at home?

Housing likely accounts for a significant portion of your income. The most common recommendation is to spend only 30 percent of your monthly take-home pay on housing.[3] However, I would guess most people spend 50 percent or more of their income on their housing costs. This is because the cost of rent and the purchase price of homes have gone up significantly in recent years.

I recommend getting creative and getting your housing costs down as low as possible. It'll take an open mind and imagination on your part. Yet changing up your housing environment could benefit both your financial life and your *lifestyle.*

If your big money goal is financial freedom, cutting housing costs can help you get there faster. Lower housing costs let you save more today and mean you'll need less passive income to maintain your financially free lifestyle.

## My Story of Downsizing

I've prioritized keeping my housing costs low throughout my adult life.

In my twenties, I lived in a converted school bus for three years. The bus cost $1,200 to buy. After that, my housing expenses dropped to less than $200 a month, the amount I paid to park on a friend's land. When adjusted for inflation to today's dollars, my rent was less than $400 per month.

Keeping my cost of housing down helped me pay off my student loans within a year of earning my bachelor's degree.

During graduate school, I lived in a four-bedroom house with three other roommates. I was the manager of the house and moved into the smallest bedroom. As a result, I was again paying less than $200 per month in rent.

After marrying my husband, Kent, we lived in a small two-bedroom house. For many years, we were only raising one kid, so our small home fit our needs.

We also had a mother-in-law unit behind our house that we rented on Airbnb for extra income. I later learned that renting out part of your home is called *house hacking*. I'll share more about house hacking later in this chapter.

Kent and I had a shared goal of quitting our jobs so we could travel more. To reach this goal, we knew our passive income had to cover our living expenses. Eventually, we realized we could reach that goal sooner if we cut our housing costs. Since we planned to travel for half the year, we moved into our mother-in-law unit, also called an accessory unit. This allowed us to rent out the main house, which paid for our mortgage, taxes, and insurance expenses. This decision effectively reduced our housing costs to zero.

A year after we started our new life of travel, we began renting out our accessory unit while we traveled. We like to take three-month trips, which is perfect for renting to traveling nurses, who usually have three-month contracts. We found our traveling nurses and other mid-term renters on furnishedfinder.com.

Looking back, if we had moved into our accessory unit and rented out our main house earlier, we could have reached financial freedom even faster.

## How Much Can You Save On Housing?

Now it's your turn. What options do you have to cut your housing expenses?

My situation is unique, but I want you to consider different ways you could save money on housing. I've listed some of these ideas below.

Reducing housing costs takes creativity, imagination, and an open mind. It takes thinking outside the box and going against what's normal.

I also recognize that many people love their homes and don't want to give them up. Or downsizing may not appeal to you, especially if you have a large family.

If this is you, or for other reasons you wish not to change up your housing situation, I understand. I encourage you to keep reading, though, because there may come a time when you're ready for a change.

If you want to stay in your current home, consider house hacking, where you rent out part of your home. You could also add a second unit to your property that you can rent out. These options could help pay for your housing costs.

If you're not comfortable renting your personal space, other options include renting garage space, an outbuilding, or other storage space. People could rent your spare storage space and store their RVs, boats, classic cars, or personal items.

Explore creative housing options like the ones listed below and see if any could work for you. Next, brainstorm ideas on your own that might work even better. Use your notebook or the companion *Her Money Rules! Financial Planner* to write down your ideas.

## Creative Housing Options

Here, I've included creative housing options for both renters and homeowners.

The options for renters include renting a smaller space or getting a roommate. If you own or are buying a home, options include adding an accessory unit or tiny home to your property. To implement some of these options, you might need to save up for a down payment or refinance an existing home.

For renters:

- Move into a smaller single-family home or a smaller apartment. Can you get by with one fewer bedroom?
- Move back in with Mom and Dad. Yeah, I know this is your least favorite idea.
- Get a roommate—or two, or three.
- Rent a studio apartment or a tiny home.
- Rent a trailer or manufactured home. Or buy a travel trailer and park it at an RV park or on a friend's property.
- Purchase a camper van and experience van life.

For homeowners:

- Get one or more roommates to help pay your mortgage.
- Turn a spare room into a short- or mid-term rental.
- If you have an accessory unit on your property, rent it to short-, mid-, or long-term renters. Or move into the smaller unit and rent out your house.
- Move a trailer, mobile home, or tiny home onto your property and rent that out. Again, another option is to move into it and rent out your house.
- Leverage the equity in your home and use it to build an accessory unit on your property. Or use your equity as a down payment on a second property you can rent out—and get into the rental business!
- Purchase a smaller home and either sell your larger home or turn it into a rental.

Americans' expectations for how much space a family needs have expanded over the past sixty years.[4] In the 1960s, my dad grew up in a three-bedroom, one-bathroom home, shared by him, his parents, and two sisters. I still wonder how they did it. It's hard for me to imagine five people sharing one bathroom.

Can you lower your expectations of how much space you need?

### Refinance or Leverage Your Home Equity

For homeowners, some options listed above require investing additional money to implement them. If you have built up some savings, you could invest those savings. Or you could open an equity line of credit or refinance your mortgage.

As I write this chapter in spring 2025, interest rates are near their highest level in recent history. The last time interest rates were this high was in the early 2000s.[5] Thus, you could wait and see if interest rates fall before using a loan to leverage your home equity.

If you choose to build an accessory unit or move a trailer or tiny home onto your property, be sure to do your research. Check your local housing code for the rules on these options.

## Beyond Housing

After implementing ways to save on housing, which is often your biggest expense, it's time to review your other large expenses.

Below are additional expense categories, along with ideas on how you can save money in each one.

- Transportation
- Healthcare
- Groceries
- Dining out
- Utilities
- Phone, data, internet
- Subscriptions
- Insurance and self-insurance
- Clothing
- Other Items

Just like with housing, cutting other expenses can help you reach your investment goals and reduce your cost of living. The more expenses you cut, and the more drastically you cut them, the faster you can reach the crossover point of financial freedom, if that's your goal.

## TRANSPORTATION

We live in a car-filled world, so most of us get around by car. Depending on your neighborhood and local planning policies, driving everywhere might be the safest or only option.

However, the cost of owning a car can be significant. If you buy a new or used car on credit, you'll have a monthly car loan expense for two to five years. Then there's the cost of gas, insurance, and maintenance.

Review your transportation needs and current costs. How are you getting to work and running errands? How much are you spending on car loans? What are your monthly gas and annual maintenance expenses? Do you spend money on parking?

Then consider the different transportation cost-cutting options included below.

### Get Rid of the Car Payment

My daughter recently got rid of a $200 a month car payment. Her car was worth about $10,000, and she still owed $7,000. She sold her car and paid off the loan. Then she used the $3,000 in equity to buy an older car that was rated reliable and had low mileage.

Do you have a car payment? If so, are you willing to make a similar tradeoff?

### Downsize to One Car

While working, my husband and I had only one car. In fact, we still get by with one daily driver. For ten years, I commuted an hour to work and was part of a vanpool. This both saved me the cost of a second car and the cost of parking. When I got a job two miles from home, I walked, biked, or rode the bus, depending on the weather.

If you're married or have a partner, do you need two cars, or can you make do with one? Do you both work outside the home and work at opposite ends of town? Could you carpool, bus, or bike to work?

### Reduce the Number of Car Trips

I'm lucky to live in a town with hundreds of miles of bike lanes and bike paths. My neighborhood is also very walkable, with the nearest grocery store within three blocks of my home. My city also has a reliable and low-cost bus service.

To reduce the number of car trips you make, are there alternative transportation options available to you? Does your town have a reliable and convenient bus system? Does your town have dedicated bike lanes?

To make fewer car trips, you could also do your weekly errands all at once or on your way home from work.

### Upgrade to a Newer, More Reliable Car

How reliable is your car? Does it require a lot of repairs and maintenance? If so, it might make sense to buy a newer, more reliable car with fewer miles, and thus fewer repair costs.

If you buy a newer car, you'll have a higher upfront cost. But you could save on repairs for the first five to ten years.

However, when shopping for a car, don't lose thousands the minute you drive it off the lot. Instead, buy a quality used car with low miles and good reliability.

Check Consumer Reports to make sure the car you're about to buy is reliable.[6] This will save you a lot on repair costs over the life of the car. Don't forget to look at gas mileage! Is the car going to get you at least thirty miles per gallon?

### Live Closer to Your Work

If you're considering downsizing your home, can you also use that opportunity to move closer to your work? Moving closer to your work means fewer miles on your car and more savings on gas and car maintenance. Or if you move close enough, you could walk, bike, or ride the bus to work.

## HEALTHCARE

Healthcare costs can either be our second or third highest expense, depending on our age and health status. These costs can include health insurance premiums, co-pays, and deductibles. Or if you don't have insurance, out-of-pocket costs.

Like car insurance or homeowner's insurance, having health insurance can save us from huge unexpected expenses. Such as expenses arising from an illness or accidental injury.

If we're young and healthy, hopefully we only need one preventative medical exam per year.

However, as we get older, the number of yearly medical appointments can grow.

To help us save on healthcare costs over our lifetime, we can prioritize our health and wellness. With few exceptions, we're all responsible for our own health. Exceptions include things like accidents, genetic conditions, or rare illnesses passed down through families.

I encourage you to prioritize your health and do everything you can to stay healthy and prevent disease.

Specifically, consider these health practices:

- Eat your fruits, cruciferous vegetables, leafy greens, beans, legumes, and whole grains.
- Brush your teeth twice a day and get your teeth cleaned once or twice a year.
- Exercise. At a minimum, walk for twenty minutes a day at a brisk pace that gets your heart rate up. To stay flexible and strong, do daily stretching and strength training.
- Get plenty of sleep and keep a consistent sleep schedule.
- Reduce and combat stress with meditation, breathing exercises, and yoga.

You didn't know this book would also be about your health, did you? It's true, taking care of your health will save you *a ton* of money down the road!

### A Special Note on the Impact of Foods on Our Health

The science gets clearer and clearer every year that sugar, ultra-processed foods, and fast foods are bad for us. These foods impair our ability to maintain good health. They're also responsible for most of the increased cases of obesity, heart disease, and diabetes in the U.S.

## Food Quality = Health Quality

There's firm evidence that processed meat causes cancer. For example, the World Health Organization considers processed meats to be a Group 1 carcinogen known to cause cancer.[7] Processed meats include lunch meat, bacon, pepperoni, and hotdogs.

If you're interested in managing your health through the foods you eat, I highly recommend you read Dr. Furhman's new book, *Eat for Life*.[8] This book includes a table ranking foods from most to least nutritious.

### GROCERIES

For many, food is possibly the second or third highest expense after housing or healthcare costs.

Groceries is the category where I've found it hardest to cut costs. However, once I started budgeting and setting a defined grocery budget, I've been better at keeping my grocery expenses down. The reason having a grocery budget works so well for me is that I'm now more mindful when I go grocery shopping. I used to plan meals while walking down the aisle, and I'd grab whatever looked good to me. This resulted in a lot of food waste. For instance, I'd buy produce for a meal, but forget to make it and find the spoiled veggies a week later.

Now, I plan my meals, create a grocery list based on those meals, and shop from my list. I avoid being tempted by snack and dessert foods not on my list, and this both helps my budget and my health.

I'm lucky to live three blocks from the grocery store, so I also shop multiple times a week instead of once a week. Shopping more often and meal planning have saved me a ton of money and food waste.

I know what staples Kent and I go through each week, so I will stock up on those when they go on sale.

## DINING OUT

Depending on your habits, dining out can be a significant expense.

Kent and I have a tradition of getting takeout every Friday night. This is an important tradition for us. However, we dine out only on special occasions like birthdays. We also indulge in our lattes and mochas only once or twice a month.

During college, I would pull out $20 from the ATM every week to cover dining out and bar money. In today's dollars, that's about $40 a week. Some weeks, I didn't even spend the whole $20. It became a game to see how much I had left at the end of the week.

Review your drinking and dining out habits. Are you mindful of how much you're eating out and how much you're spending?

It's important that we treat ourselves now and again, as this can be a source of joy in our lives. Yet we want to have a conscious plan for treating ourselves. If you haven't already, make a plan for how many times each week or month you'll dine out and get coffee to-go or takeout. Then commit to sticking with that plan.

Another big dining out expense can be lunches out on the days you work in the office. What's your lunch routine? When you work at the office away from home, do you eat lunch out every day or do you pack lunch?

If you're eating lunch out most days, this can be a significant cost. In my experience, the cost of lunch at an inexpensive restaurant is between $10 and $15. At an average of twenty work days a month, that could add up to $200 to $300 per month.

During my working days, I would eat out about once a month. Mostly, I would bring a can of soup, a frozen meal, leftovers, or a big salad. I also had snacks on hand, so I wasn't running to the vending machine every afternoon during my afternoon slump.

Saving money on dining out can add up to a lot of savings, and it can also make you healthier. Cooking from scratch can be a lot healthier than eating out, where you don't have control over how much oil, sugar, or salt is in the food.

## UTILITIES

Utilities include other housing costs like electricity, gas, water, and garbage service. If you're renting and your rent includes utilities, then you won't have to worry too much about cutting these costs. However, if your rent does not include utilities or you own your own home, there are opportunities to save.

Here are some tips for saving on utilities:

### Garbage

- If your garbage service offers different-sized garbage cans at different prices, choose the smallest one and reduce your waste.
- If there's recycling in your area, learn what's recyclable and sort it out of your garbage.
- Get a trash compactor or use your own effort to flatten containers and compact your waste. One thing I do to help compact my waste is I cut up the plastic rectangle salad containers before throwing them away.

### Heating and Cooling

- Learn the ideal temperatures for comfort and savings. For example, 68°F in the cold months and 78°F in the summer.
- Program your thermostat based on the times of day you're at home, at work, and sleeping.
- Look for any drafts coming in from windows or doors, and insulate them.
- Close any vents and doors in rooms you rarely use or when you'll be away from home, such as during work hours.

### Water

- If you have a dishwasher, use that instead of handwashing dishes.
- Keep your showers short and turn the water off while soaping up or shampooing your hair.
- If you can get away with it, stop watering your grass. If you own your home, transition from grass to other landscape options that don't need water.

## PHONE, DATA, AND INTERNET

We live in an internet and data-connected world. However, with this connection comes a lot of cost. At home, most of us have an internet service provider. Most of us also have smartphones with data plans.

Unless you're locked into a contract, or once your contract is over, shop around often for lower-cost plans with similar speed and quality.

Fiber-optic internet recently came to my neighborhood, and I now spend 50 percent less than when I had cable internet. Depending on where you live, you too might save if you switch.

There are also more options now for cell phone and data service with similar quality and coverage as the big carriers. Shop around to find the best deal for your data needs. There are some providers with a low-cost monthly fee, and yet the same high-speed unlimited data coverage.

## SUBSCRIPTIONS

Ah, yes, subscriptions. It's interesting to see all the new banking apps out there to help us manage our subscriptions. We might have shopping, news, magazine, music, game, and streaming subscriptions. The number of our subscriptions can become overwhelming, and the cost can add up. Thus, it's important to review our subscriptions regularly and ensure we're still getting entertainment and value.

Kent and I finally cut the cable cord about seven years ago, but we still have Kindle Unlimited and Amazon Prime. We've also had temporary subscriptions to other streaming platforms, depending on what we're interested in watching. Sometimes I'll sign up for a promotional rate and cancel before the increase.

I review my subscriptions often to ensure we're still using them and that they're worth the cost. When I first sign up for a service with a temporary discount, I put a reminder on my calendar to cancel before it goes to full price.

When I go to cancel a subscription, the provider often offers a discount to continue. So, even if I want to keep a subscription, I try canceling and see if I can score a discount.

Now, it's your turn. Review all your monthly cable or digital subscriptions, and have an honest assessment of how much of each service you use. Keep the services you enjoy and get rid of the subscriptions you don't use. Another option is to set a budget for entertainment. Then prioritize the services you use and keep your highest priority services until you reach your target budget amount.

Besides digital subscriptions, determine what other subscriptions you have. Ask yourself if you need these or if they're luxuries you can live without. Can you cut magazine subscriptions, box subscriptions, or sample subscriptions?

Also, review your gym membership. Do you have a gym membership that you use at least two times a week? Or do you find yourself too busy or prefer to work out at home or outside? If you're using your gym membership and you're reaping the benefits, then keep it. If not, consider letting it go and saving the expense.

## INSURANCE AND SELF-INSURANCE

Insurance can help protect our assets and can also be required if you have a car loan or a home mortgage.

It's important not to be underinsured, so we can protect our assets. However, it's just as important not to be overinsured, which means you're paying for insurance you don't need.

To save money, you want to be insured just enough and use self-insurance as much as you can.

### What Does It Mean to Be Self-Insured?

Being self-insured means having enough savings to cover unexpected expenses that insurance would normally take care of. For example, instead of buying warranty insurance, you could use your own savings to repair or replace a broken electronic device or appliance. Choosing a high insurance deductible is another form of self-insurance. If your comprehensive car insurance has a $1,000 deductible, you would pay out of pocket for any damage costing less than that amount.

You can gradually become more self-insured by growing your emergency fund. A larger emergency fund allows you to choose a higher deductible, which lowers your insurance premiums and saves you money.

### What is a Deductible?

Your deductible is the amount you would owe to cover the cost of an insurance claim. Suppose you have comprehensive car insurance with a $500 deductible. In case of an accident, you would need to have $500 in savings to cover the deductible. If an accident caused $1,700 in damage to your car, you would pay $500 and your insurance company would cover the remaining $1,200.

Eventually, you want your emergency fund to be large enough to cover the highest possible insurance deductible for your vehicle and home. Some car insurance providers offer a $2,000 deductible. Depending on your home loan and homeowner's insurance provider, you could have a deductible as high as $10,000.

When I increased my homeowner's insurance deductible to $10,000, the maximum my mortgage allowed, I saved $400 per year on my annual premium.

### Self-Insured for Healthcare

Just like car and home insurance, you could be self-insured for healthcare by having enough savings to purchase a high-deductible health plan. This would save you money on your health insurance premium. For example, you could choose to grow a health savings fund of $10,000. In that case, you'd only have to pay for catastrophic health insurance, which has annual deductibles of $9,000 on average. After the deductible, catastrophic health insurance covers much of your remaining healthcare costs, such as hospital stays and care for significant injuries or illnesses. Before you have met the deductible, you will pay out of pocket whenever you need to go to the doctor.

However, I'm cautious about being self-insured for healthcare. You never know when a devastating accident or illness will occur that could cost you much more than $10,000.

## Say No to Extended Warranties

Another example of self-insurance is not buying extended warranties on household goods, appliances, or electronics.

Usually, when you purchase an appliance or electronic device, you're asked if you want to pay for an extended warranty. These warranties can cost another 20 to 30 percent based on the purchase price. Usually, manufacturer warranties guarantee appliances and devices for one year. An extended warranty protects the appliance or device from a manufacturer's defect for another year or two.

Also, say no to car or home repair insurance. These insurance products charge you a monthly fee and promise to pay for maintenance and repair costs after you've paid the deductible. The cost of a car repair insurance plan can cost between $65 and $140 per month.[9] The deductibles for these plans can be between $100 and $250.[10]

Besides the high monthly cost, extended warranties or repair insurance often require a lot of your time and effort before they actually pay off. Thus, it's often not worth the headache, let alone the cost.

## CLOTHING

Depending on your personality, you may spend a lot or a little on clothing. You could be as extreme in your wardrobe as Steve Jobs was and have the same outfit of blue jeans and a black t-shirt. Or you might love fashion and shop for the latest trends.

I'm not as extreme as Steve Jobs was, but I definitely wear my favorite three outfits most of the time. I've never enjoyed clothes shopping and only shop when I need something, like replacing my favorite pair of jeans when they wear out.

If you're into fashion, and you love shopping for new outfits, review how much you spend each month. Have you been mindlessly spending on clothes? If so, try a more mindful approach. Come up with a monthly budget amount that both fits your love of shopping, but also allows you to meet your other budget goals.

When you see a piece of clothing that you absolutely love, have a rule that you'll sleep on it. If you wake up the next day and you're still thinking about it and still want it, then purchase it. This rule works because you'll often realize that you don't really want or need that item. You can apply this rule to any purchase.

In addition, beware of sales and understand the psychology of sales. To get you in the door, retail marketers use psychology when they come up with discounts and sale percentages. Retailers often mark up clothing prices significantly. They use sales to make you think you're getting a good deal. For example, if a jeans store has a buy-one-get-one 50 percent off sale, you're only saving 25 percent off the total purchase. And do you really need two pairs of jeans?

## Save 100 percent when you buy nothing.[11]

If you need a clothing item, shop for that item. When you do, shop for the best quality, so you know the item will last. Shop around for the best price, so you don't have to pay more than you need to.

If you use shopping for entertainment or to spend quality time with someone you care about, set a budget for the day. To decide on your clothing budget for the day, I recommend you review your spending goals and monthly budget for clothing. Then, make it a game to find the best items for the amount you have to spend.

### OTHER ITEMS

Americans love to shop and own gadgets and equipment. However, before buying that next gadget, consider how much you'll use that item.

Do you really *need* that thing?

Let's say you're considering buying home exercise equipment, such as a treadmill. Are you sure you'll actually use it? If yes, consider buying a used one. You can always upgrade to the new model if you end up using it all the time.

Think twice about buying one-off appliances, such as a hot dog toaster, crepe pan, or cake pop maker. These are things you'll probably rarely use. When deciding to buy something, ask yourself how often you'll use it. Will another item you already own work instead?

For items you need or that would bring you great joy or entertainment, do your research and find brands that are reliable. Invest in a Consumer Reports subscription. This is one subscription I recommend when shopping for anything over $300. But then cancel your monthly subscription as soon as you've made your decision.

## EXTREME EXPENSE CUTTING

If you want to get super serious about cutting expenses and reach your big financial goal sooner, try *extreme expense cutting.* I may have made up this term, but the FIRE movement inspired it.

FIRE stands for Financial Independence Retire Early.

The FIRE movement inspired people to cut their living expenses as low as possible to enable them to retire as soon as possible. The idea is to cut your spending and make sacrifices until you're able to save a targeted percentage of your income.

My favorite FIRE blog is mrmoneymustache.com by Peter Adeney. I shared Peter's story in the last chapter. On his blog, Peter shares stories and examples of extreme expense cutting. For example, not buying things new and instead getting them for free online. Another example is hypermiling, which is where you squeeze as many miles as you can out of a gallon of gas. Being hyper-focused on accelerating smoothly, braking less, and coasting when you can will help you lower your gas mileage.[12] And of course, riding your bike or the bus, and only driving when absolutely necessary.

Other extreme expense-cutting ideas include line drying your clothes, taking quick showers, turning the heat down, and cooking from scratch.

## KEY POINTS

- We save money and build wealth only when our living expenses are less than our income.
- You can significantly reduce your living expenses by cutting your largest expenses, such as housing, transportation, healthcare, and food.
- Because housing is your biggest expense, it's important to find creative ways of reducing this expense, such as by downsizing or house hacking.
- Other ideas for saving money include cooking from scratch, rarely eating out, cutting subscriptions, reducing utility costs, and not buying things new. And being insured just enough—not over-insured or under-insured—and using self-insurance as much as you can.

## ACTION PLAN

In the companion *Her Money Rules! Financial Planner*, or your notebook, complete the following action steps:

- ☐ Think about and write at least three alternative housing options you would consider and reasonably implement to save money on housing. Choose one that you could implement in the next few months to a year.
- ☐ Think about and write at least five alternative transportation options for cutting your monthly transportation expenses. Choose and commit to one or more of these options.

- ▢ Including housing and transportation, list out all your current living expenses and track or estimate monthly amounts for each item or expense category. For annual expenses, divide by twelve to turn them into monthly amounts. Use the Monthly Personal Expense Worksheet in the companion *Her Money Rules! Financial Planner* or download and print additional copies of the worksheet at hermoneyrules.com/bonus.
- ▢ Add up your current actual living expenses and compare the total to your average monthly income after taxes. Evaluate and write your current financial status: 1) Your income exceeds your monthly living expenses (you're living within your means), or 2) Your income is less than your monthly living expenses (you're not living within your means and at risk of accruing debt).

## COMING UP IN RULE 4: CREATE YOUR PERFECT BUDGET

Budgeting is essential for being thoughtful with our money, living within our means, and achieving our big financial goals. In the next chapter, you'll learn the key principles of budgeting and the step-by-step process for creating your own perfect budget.

# RULE 4

# CREATE YOUR PERFECT BUDGET

*"Do not save what is left after spending, but spend what is left after saving."*
*—Warren Buffett*[1]

## MOM'S ENVELOPE BUDGET

As a kid, I remember my mom paying cash for groceries from a plain white envelope. I asked Mom about it, and she explained her budgeting method to me. She and my dad would agree on an amount each month for the household budget. My mom would withdraw that amount in cash at the beginning of the month and divide it between groceries, gas, and other purchases.

I didn't give it much thought back then. We always seemed to have plenty of food in the house. Mom would also budget money for other purchases, such as new softball cleats, because I outgrew my old pair.

I always seemed to have what I needed for school and sports. I got new school clothes at the beginning of each school year, and my parents paid for sports fees and other after-school activities. However, I understood we weren't a rich family. We weren't rich, but we weren't poor either.

As I got older, my parents shared their financial goals with me. I learned my parents had an aggressive goal to save up for their retirement, and most of their income went to that goal. I remember thinking, *Huh, we really are rich, we just don't live like it!*

## MY FIRST BUDGET

Even with the example my mom provided, I resisted creating my own monthly budget. I tracked my expenses and never spent more than I earned, so I didn't think I needed to.

One justification I had for not budgeting was that I'm naturally more of a saver than a spender. When I spent money, it was on the things I needed, like groceries, work clothes, and home supplies.

However, I decided it was time to budget when I was three years from reaching my big financial goal. I knew that reaching my goal of financial freedom depended on keeping my monthly living expenses at or below my investment or passive income.

### Saving $400 My First Month

When I was ready to create my first budget, I found the app You Need a Budget, now known as YNAB.[2] They offer a free trial period, so I tested it out for a month and ended up loving it. This app made it easy to set up my budget, record my purchases, and track it throughout the month.

Because I kept track of my family's spending and knew what our fixed expenses were, it didn't take long to create my first monthly budget. For non-fixed expenses, I averaged out what I'd been spending on things like groceries and gas.

Once I started budgeting, my biggest surprise was how much money I saved on groceries and other purchases. I saved a whopping $400 that first month.

Visualize me kicking myself as I realized I potentially could have achieved financial freedom sooner had I started budgeting sooner.

### Being Mindful of My Spending

I became more mindful of my spending thanks to budgeting. In particular, having a grocery budget made me more mindful each time I went to the grocery store. I started getting better at meal planning and purchased only items on my list. Unless it was on sale, I also stopped stocking up on things.

Then, as I neared the end of the month and my remaining budget got smaller, I focused on squeezing even more. I would shop only for the bare minimum until the first of the month, when my budget would start over again.

If you're like me, I hated the idea of having a budget. The first thing that came to mind was scarcity. Why would I want to create scarcity for myself by having a budget? However, I'm now convinced and love budgeting. It helps that apps like YNAB make it easy and also gamify it for me.

I now know that budgeting is a *must* for being thoughtful with my spending, living within my means, and reaching my big financial goals.

## IMPORTANT BUDGETING PRINCIPLES

Before creating your own budget, I'd like to introduce you to seven important budgeting principles. Keep these in mind while developing and working toward your perfect budget.

## 1. Create a Spending Plan

To create a budget that accounts for all your financial goals, current and future, it helps to create an overarching spending plan. Use the 50/30/20 rule to divide your after-tax income into three categories: 50 percent to needs, 30 percent to wants, and 20 percent to savings.[3] This rule helps you keep a balance between spending on core needs, life's pleasures, and financial security. Needs would include housing, food, transportation, utilities, and insurance. Entertainment, travel, and fashion are examples of wants. The savings category would include emergency fund savings, investments, and debt repayment.

A similar rule is to divide your income into four categories:

- Live: 50 to 70 percent for both needs and wants
- Grow: 15 to 20 percent for savings and investments
- Owe: 10 to 20 percent for debt repayment
- Give: 3 to 5 percent for charitable donations[4]

Use these two rules as guidance for creating your own spending plan. Whether you have three or four categories, create a spending plan that fits with your lifestyle and goals. Then use your overall spending plan as a guide to create your detailed monthly budget.

## 2. Give Every Dollar a Job

The most important principle of budgeting is giving every dollar a job. Giving every dollar a job helps you prioritize spending and prevents overspending. To do this, you assign each dollar you receive from a paycheck or other income source to a specific expense or category of spending.[5]

Without a budget, our income waits for us to spend it. We also err in placing our trust in our account balance. We risk seeing our balance after getting paid and feeling flush. Then, we may decide we have plenty of money, and it's okay to spend on spontaneous purchases.

Having a budget where we assign each dollar a job as it arrives creates a more mindful way of spending. It also ensures we're paying our bills on time and prioritizing our spending and savings for other financial goals. We can pay our bills, plan for the future, and budget for fun and entertainment, all without guilt.

If you budget $50 for entertainment, that money now has a job. You don't have to feel bad about spending it, or worry you're overspending, because you allocated it for that purpose.

### 3. Use Last Month's Paycheck for This Month's Bills

Instead of living paycheck to paycheck, *use last month's paycheck for this month's bills*. This is also called the *month ahead* strategy, or living on last month's income.[6] This strategy is critical for financial stability and ensures you only spend money you've already earned.

Living on last month's income may not be possible for your first budget. However, it's important that you work toward this and make this your first savings goal.

When you're spending money you earned last month, you create a built-in buffer. Instead of having a stack of bills waiting on your earned money, you'll have a stack of money waiting for the bills to come in. This gives you certainty that you'll have the cash you need to cover your expenses. You're not waiting for the next paycheck to cover your bills, which means less stress. Less stress means better physical and mental health and more peace of mind.

Another benefit of using last month's income for this month's expenses is that it stops the living paycheck-to-paycheck cycle. Living paycheck to paycheck means that every time you get paid, you need that money for immediate expenses, including bills that are due or past due. In contrast, using last month's income allows you to have the money ready when bills are due. Using last month's income also helps you avoid late fees and a damaged credit score.

If you're paid twice a month, you might have to use your entire second paycheck to pay rent. This leaves the next paycheck for other bills and food, and makes you vulnerable to financial emergencies. Using last month's income breaks this cycle by creating a buffer.

When you have a buffer, you can better plan for the future and create a safety net. If you know your income from last month is meeting your immediate bills and expenses, you'll have greater confidence to save and invest.

### 4. Pay Yourself First

*Paying yourself first* is the practice of budgeting money for savings, investments, and debt repayments before allocating money to other bills and expenses. This also includes setting up automatic withholdings from your paycheck or transfers from your checking account to fund savings, investments, or debt accounts. Automation removes the spending decision by automatically transferring the money before you even see it. Otherwise, you'll want to transfer these dollars manually on the very first day of each month.

The concept of *paying yourself first* could be the most difficult to understand, especially if you're stuck in the paycheck-to-paycheck cycle. You may ask yourself, *How can I pay myself first when I'm late paying my phone bill and I still need to scrape up rent for next month*?

Let's assume you've reached the point where you can use last month's income to cover the current month's expenses. At that point, it's time to assign a certain number of those dollars to *paying yourself first* before assigning those dollars elsewhere. Otherwise, it's easy to spend our money on other wants like eating out, entertainment, or fashion.

Paying ourselves first also honors our spending plan and our financial goals. Remember the big financial goal you created for yourself in Rule 2? By consistently setting aside money for your future, you're actively working towards your financial aspirations rather than only covering immediate expenses.

*Paying yourself first* also puts you in the habit of living within your means. You set aside money for your savings goals and then you allocate the rest to the lifestyle you can afford.

In addition, paying ourselves first helps our money work for us. The sooner you save and invest, the sooner your money will benefit from the power of compound interest. By starting to save and invest early, you give your money more time to grow, potentially increasing your wealth significantly over the long term.

Have I convinced you? How much of your income can you use to *pay yourself first* to put yourself on the path of reaching your big financial goal?

## 5. Fixed versus Variable Expenses

Fixed expenses are expenses that don't change from month to month, like rent, insurance premiums, and subscription fees. These fixed expenses are easy to budget for because they rarely change, and you can carry them forward in your budget from month to month.

Variable expenses are costs that vary each month, such as groceries, gas, and dining out. You have more control over how much you spend on these expenses. The more you practice budgeting and tracking your variable expenses, the easier it becomes to predict and budget for them in the future.

## 6. Non-Monthly Expenses

As you create your first budget, you'll want to be aware of any annual or semiannual expenses. These non-monthly expenses can include annual insurance premiums, birthday and holiday gifts, home repairs, or an annual vacation.

Non-monthly expenses can catch us off guard and throw a wrench into our perfect budget if we don't plan for them.

The best way to handle these non-monthly expenses is to break them down into smaller monthly budget items. To illustrate, if you have an Amazon Prime membership billed at $139 a year, then you'd budget $11.60 a month in your Prime Membership category. Then, when this annual bill is due, you already have the money set aside to pay it.

However, if you have a non-monthly expense under $20, you can probably use your "Stuff I Forgot to Budget For" category to cover it. Learn more about this category in the next principle.

### 7. Build in Flexibility

Remember, even the best-laid plans can often go awry. Thus, it's important to build flexibility and contingencies into your budget.

This is *your* budget, and *you* get to decide where each dollar goes. Maybe you run out of money in one category and still need or want to make a purchase in that category. When this happens, you can choose to move money over from another category to cover it.

I learned from the folks at YNAB to create a category called "Stuff I Forgot to Budget For." This category is for one-off or unexpected expenses that pop up.[7] Unexpected expenses could include gifts, car repairs, or medical bills. Even though you budget for unexpected expenses, it's important to categorize the actual expenses in the right category. For instance, a graduation gift for your niece would get categorized under "Gifts." You then move the money out of the "Stuff I Forgot to Budget For" category into the "Gifts" category.

My practice is to put 5 percent of my budget into this category, and it has saved my *butt*, I mean *budget*, many times. I chose 5 percent because that gives me about $150 of wiggle room on my $2800 budget. After years of budgeting, I still use this buffer for unexpected bills and needed purchases. I also have an emergency savings fund for big unexpected expenses.

Also, keep in mind, not every month's budget is going to be the same. You'll want to update your budget whenever your priorities shift or when you have changes in income, expenses, or goals.

## CREATE YOUR PERFECT BUDGET

To create your perfect budget, use the Monthly Budget Worksheet in the companion *Her Money Rules! Financial Planner* or download it at hermoneyrules.com/bonus. As you're building your budget, use the seven budgeting principles for guidance.

### Create a Spending Plan:

- Decide how you'll allocate your income by percent to overarching spending categories, such as needs and wants (Live), savings (Grow), debt repayment (Owe), and giving (Give). The total should add up to 100 percent.
- Your spending plan should factor in your financial goals and your current lifestyle.
- Use your spending plan as a guide for building your detailed monthly budget.
- Record your spending plan on your One-Page Financial Plan.

### Give Every Dollar a Job:

- Determine your total income from the prior month, including income from your paychecks, tips, side hustles, or other sources. Use this amount to create a budget for the coming month.

- Knowing your total income will help you create a zero-based budget, where you budget every dollar, including the dollars you budget for savings or investments.
- If you receive unexpected income or money, such as cash gifts, you want to assign those dollars to a budget category as well. Even if it's your "Fun and Entertainment" category.

### Use Last Month's Paycheck for This Month's Bills:

- To *use last month's paycheck to pay for this month's bills,* you would use your total after-tax income as the basis of your next month's budget.
- If you're not able to do this because you've already spent some or all of last month's income, there are a few options. You could use a combination of any savings you have and only budget for basic needs in the first month. If this still doesn't get you a *month ahead* after your first month of budgeting, you'll need to make this your first savings goal. Calculate your monthly living expenses to determine how much you need for your "Month Ahead" savings fund. For example, let's assume your monthly living expenses total $2,000. If you can save $500 a month, then it'll take you four months to save enough to cover a month's worth of expenses.

### Pay Yourself First:

- Before assigning dollars to other budget categories, first assign dollars to your "Month Ahead" savings fund or emergency savings fund. Once you've met those savings goals, you would first assign dollars to other savings, debt repayment, or investments in future months. What you assign is based on your spending plan and your savings and investment goals.
- At the beginning of each month, immediately transfer the money out of your checking account into the relevant savings, debt, or investment account.

### Fixed versus Variable Expenses:

- After determining your estimated income, and *paying yourself first*, you can now assign your dollars to other expense items. Create a list of all your expenses and current monthly amounts.
- The next step is to look at every expense and expense category, and set budget targets for each. For this first-draft budget, fill in your fixed expenses and your average variable expenses.
- Then review every expense item and category, and determine if you can reduce or cut that item. For each expense, ask yourself, how important is this?
- For some fixed expenses like rent and mortgage payments, you won't be able to reduce those right away. However, you might have monthly fixed expenses like digital subscriptions that you can review. You can also choose to cut variable expenses like groceries. You could cut these by 10 percent, for instance.

### Non-Monthly Expenses:

- You also want to ensure you create budget categories and assign dollars in your monthly budget for non-monthly expenses, like annual subscription dues and vacations.
- Estimate the total amount for these non-monthly expenses, and divide by the number of months left before you need the money for these expenses. Add that number to your monthly budget until you've fully funded that expense. For instance, let's say you're planning a week-long trip to the Oregon coast, with a budget of $1,500. You plan the trip for August, and you add it to your monthly budget starting in February. That gives you six months to budget and save $250 per month for the trip.

### Build in Flexibility:

- You can create some wiggle room in your budget by using a category like "Stuff I Forgot to Budget For." The percentage you decide will depend on your total income, expenses, and goals.
- Remember, you can be flexible as you work through your budget during the month. If you overspend in one category, you can transfer money from another category.

## FINE-TUNE YOUR BUDGET

Every month, review your past month's budget for actual income and expenses. It's important to look back on the past month to see which expense categories you might have overestimated or underestimated. Then, make changes and fine-tune your budget each month as you practice the art of budgeting.

As you review the past month, perhaps you realize your grocery budget needs to be bigger. But you see other categories you can cut to make up for it. Or maybe you've become more confident and successful at saving money with your budget, and you can increase your savings category.

After a few months, you could also look at your necessary expenses versus your wants. What percentage of your monthly budget goes toward necessary expenses, wants, debt repayment, and savings? Decide if you want to change these percentages. Unless you make big lifestyle changes, your necessary spending may not change, but you could change the percentage between wants, debt, and savings.

As you implement strategies to cut your biggest expenses, like housing, you can adjust your budget and assign more dollars to savings or debt repayment.

## USE A BUDGETING APP

As you build or fine-tune your budget, make budgeting easier and fun by using a budget tool or app. YNAB is my favorite because it is user-friendly.[8] I also love it for its emphasis on budgeting income after you receive it, instead of planning or budgeting future income. The app also focuses on assigning each dollar a job, also called zero-based budgeting. This means you assign every dollar you earn to a saving or spending category.

Here are three other popular budget tools you can try:

- EveryDollar is a zero-based budget tool designed by Ramsey Solutions, personal finance expert Dave Ramsey's company.[9] You can categorize expenses and receive custom reports and recommendations based on your spending habits.
- Goodbudget helps you plan expenses using the envelope budgeting system.[10] Users can allocate their income into digital envelopes named for different spending categories.
- Honeydue is designed for budgeting with a partner.[11] In this app, you and your partner can create custom expense categories and set up monthly limits on each. The app alerts you when you or your partner are nearing the monthly limit. This tool places more of an emphasis on reflecting on past spending than on planning for future expenses.

Most of these apps let you easily record your spending as you go. I have a habit of recording every purchase I make, even before leaving the store. So I don't forget and overspend the next day.

If you love spreadsheets or paper budgets, that's fine too. But remember to save your receipts and subtract from your categories at the end of each day to avoid overspending.

## KEY POINTS

- Budgeting is a *must* for being mindful and thoughtful with our spending, living within our means, and reaching our big financial goals.
- Giving every dollar that comes your way a job and assigning it to a spending category will help you prioritize spending.
- The budget strategy of *using last month's paycheck for this month's bills* is critical for financial stability and ensures you only spend money you've already earned.
- The budget strategy of *paying yourself first* puts you in the habit of living within your means.

## ACTION PLAN

In the companion *Her Money Rules! Financial Planner*, or your notebook, complete the following action steps:

- ☐ Decide how you'll allocate your income by percent to overarching spending categories, such as needs and wants (Live), savings (Grow), debt repayment (Owe), and giving (Give). The total should add up to 100 percent. Record your spending plan on your One-Page Financial Plan found in the *Her Money Rules! Financial Planner.*
- ☐ Create your perfect budget. Use your spending plan as a guide for building your detailed monthly budget. Make sure you have a zero-sum budget, which means your total budget equals your total estimated after-tax income for the month. Use the seven budgeting

principles described above. You can download and print extra copies of the Monthly Budget Worksheet at hermoneyrules.com/bonus.

- [ ] Once you've created your perfect budget, create a way to track your budget. One option is to download your free trial of YNAB and enter and track your budget there. Or you can use another budgeting tool of your choice, like EveryDollar, Goodbudget, or Honeydue. Or you can download and use the Budget Tracking Spreadsheet found in the *Her Money Rules! Financial Planner* and at hermoneyrules.com/bonus.

## COMING UP IN RULE 5: GROW YOUR INCOME AND CREATE MULTIPLE INCOME STREAMS

In Rule 3 and 4, you learned how to cut your biggest expenses and create your perfect budget. The next step toward achieving your big financial goal is to grow your income. In Rule 5, you'll learn how you can grow your income by both increasing job earnings and creating additional streams of income.

# RULE 5

# GROW YOUR INCOME AND CREATE MULTIPLE INCOME STREAMS

*"Income seldom will exceed your own personal development."*
*—Jim Rohn*[1]

## A STORY OF RAGS TO RICHES

Born in 1930, my grandmother Theora grew up poor during the Great Depression. Her father was a corn farmer in Kansas. Grandma spent her early years living in a soddy, a house built from grass sod and dirt floors.

In the late 1950s, my grandparents saved up enough money to buy a service station. My grandfather was a car mechanic and managed the fuel pumps and mechanic work, while my grandmother handled the bookkeeping. They poured all the service station's earnings into getting the business up and running. During those early days, my mother remembers a day when she only had a heel of bread and pancake syrup to eat.

Once the service station began generating a good income, my grandparents continued to invest any extra money into it and other businesses. Both of them had a desire to work hard to get themselves out of poverty. They learned that starting and owning your own business was more likely to lead them to wealth than working for someone else. Later, as their businesses grew profitable, they created a goal of retiring as millionaires.

My grandmother proved to be smart with money, and she thought like an entrepreneur. She also understood the power of multiple income streams. Before retiring, my grandparents had income from at least five businesses.

In the early 1970s, my grandparents purchased a large piece of land. On this land, they built a service shop with a used car lot, eight storage units, and a two-story building. The building had three commercial offices on the ground floor, and they used the top-floor apartment as their home.

Occasionally, my grandparents would also bid on abandoned storage units. They were bidding on storage units decades before the reality show *Storage Wars*.

My grandparents' story is the perfect example of a *rags to riches* story. They went from growing up poor during the Great Depression to retiring as millionaires.

Besides doing well at income generation, they were also savvy savers. I chuckle whenever I remember my grandfather's story of my grandmother regularly moving money from their business checking account to a savings account.

My grandfather would need money to purchase supplies and saw the low account balance. He would work long hours to get a job done sooner or take on more work, so he'd have the money he needed. I love this story because it shows both how driven my grandmother was to save money and how driven my grandfather was to earn money.

My grandparents knew what it was like to be poor. Yet instead of having a poor mindset, they believed if they worked hard, they wouldn't have to be poor again. Because they grew up during the Great Depression, they also had a frugal mindset. They didn't spend money they didn't have, and rather than spend extra money, they chose to re-invest it.

The biggest lessons I learned from my grandparents:

- Be determined and unstoppable in reaching your goals.
- Keep your expenses low.
- Take smart, calculated risks.
- Always look for ways to invest money for profit.
- Have multiple income streams.

My grandparents' big financial goal was to retire as millionaires, and they were unwavering in reaching that goal. They knew their destination, and they did whatever they could throughout their journey to wealth.

In the remaining sections of this chapter, I'll share ways you can maximize your earnings, invest in yourself, and create multiple income streams.

## MAXIMIZE LIFETIME EARNINGS

To maximize your lifetime earnings, focus on increasing your current income by building valuable skills, demonstrating your worth, and negotiating well. Because the higher your salary is now, the higher it will be at the peak of your career.

Your current wage or salary is important because it serves as the baseline for future raises and cost-of-living adjustments. A higher starting salary means that all your future percentage-based raises will also be larger.

Having a higher starting salary creates a compounding effect. This is because over the course of your working life, even minor differences in wages or salary can affect your total lifetime earnings. For example, a 5 percent increase on a $50,000 starting salary will lead to a $2,500 annual raise. This compares to a $2,250 annual raise on a $45,000 starting salary. Assuming an average raise of 5 percent each year over a thirty-year career, starting at $50,000 instead of $45,000 makes a big difference. It can add up to about $330,000 more in lifetime earnings.

The higher your current and future income, the more you're able to save and invest, and the sooner you'll reach your big financial goals.

Thus, it's important to always negotiate your starting wage or salary whenever you're hired at a new position or organization. Since you're potentially already in that first job or subsequent jobs, it may be beneficial to negotiate a raise. Or it may be favorable to seek a new job at another organization.

Negotiating wages and raises is probably one of your least favorite things to do. To set yourself up for success in negotiating raises and salaries, do your research, understand your value, practice your pitch, hold your ground, and be confident.

## INVEST IN YOURSELF

Another way to maximize your lifetime earning potential is to invest in your professional growth and go after those promotions.

Most people invest in themselves at the beginning of their careers. By working toward college certificates or degrees, becoming apprentices, or a mix of education and on-the-job training, you're investing in yourself. However, our investment in ourselves shouldn't stop there.

Continue investing in your development throughout your career with additional training, mentoring, and coaching. Become a lifelong learner.

If you're an entrepreneur or running your own business, you probably see the importance of investing in yourself. If you work for an employer, it's also worthwhile to have an entrepreneurial mindset and view your career as a business.

As you invest in improving your skills and developing new ones, seek promotion opportunities. You have the option of developing your technical skills, leadership skills, or both. Either path will lead to greater income.

If you choose to develop your leadership skills and go after supervisor or manager positions, you'll boost your earning potential. Because each step up in leadership usually comes with a higher salary.

I encourage you to *lean in.*[2] Go after that promotion even if you believe you're not 100 percent qualified. If you don't succeed the first time, keep trying, and don't give up.

I previously recounted my three attempts before being promoted to my first leadership role. Success often takes multiple attempts and requires an unstoppable mindset.

If you know you're ready for a promotion, but you keep getting overlooked by your current employer, it may be time to move on. Have the courage to look for opportunities at other organizations.

## SIDE HUSTLE YOUR WAY TO MULTIPLE INCOME STREAMS

As you grow in your job and increase your income, you can boost your income further by creating additional sources outside of work.

Earlier in this chapter, I shared the story of my grandparents and their example of creating multiple streams of income. They had five different sources of income: the mechanic business, storage unit rentals, commercial office rentals, used car sales, and storage unit auction sales.

Like my grandparents, you too can have a mix of income sources. You can set up sources of passive income or start one or more side-hustle businesses.

Sources of passive income include rents from property, royalties from books or music, or earnings from a business or stock investment. Passive income takes time and effort to set up, but once it's running, it provides steady earnings with little ongoing work.

A side hustle is a business you run outside your regular job to earn extra income. Examples of side hustle businesses include freelance writing or web design, selling products online, or driving for a rideshare company.

Start with one idea first and build from there. Keep in mind that you may not find success with your first idea. Most successful side hustlers try different things and rely on effort, persistence, and grit.

### Passive Income Options

Creating an additional income stream from a passive income source may require a financial investment, such as buying real estate to generate rental income. Owning a rental property is a form of passive income because once you have a property ready to rent, it earns you income with little additional effort.

Thanks to the sharing economy, you can now rent out a variety of other assets. Besides renting a room in your house, you can now rent out your car, boat, RV, and even your bicycle. I've also come across opportunities for renting out your swimming pool, or your backyard as a place for other people's dogs to hang out. You can also rent out smaller items like camping gear, sports equipment, and lawn tools.

There are also income stream options that don't require purchasing and owning something you rent. However, they could require a lot of time on your part. For example, you could share your skills by creating an online course, starting an affiliate marketing blog, or writing and self-publishing a book.

Writing a book takes time, but the royalties from that book can become a form of passive income. The same is true for an online course or affiliate marketing blog. With a blog, you can promote products or services and earn a commission when readers make purchases using your affiliate links.

Besides books, courses, or blogs, you could write or design other digital products to sell online. You create the product once, and then every time it sells, you'll get money deposited into your bank account.

### Side Hustle Business Options

Instead of making passive income from assets you own or create, you could put your spare time into a side hustle. A side hustle could be a business that you create, or you could contract your time with another business.

The gig economy has created many opportunities to make extra cash on the side. You could drive for a rideshare company, deliver food or groceries, or do other people's laundry. You could be a freelancer and do computer or technical-based work through sites like Upwork and Fiverr.

Another option is to create a service business such as housecleaning, furniture assembly, or car detailing. You can list these businesses on sites like Thumbtack[3] or Taskrabbit[4].

As you're thinking about products or services you can sell, I highly recommend you read the book *Acres of Diamonds* by Russell H. Conwell.[5] The key to having a successful business is finding out what people need and then filling that need.

I've only touched on a fraction of the possibilities out there for earning extra money on the side. You can find tons of other ideas on the web by searching for the terms *side hustle* or *passive income.* I also recommend the *Side Hustle School* Podcast.[6]

## KEY POINTS

- The more you maximize your current and lifetime income and invest that extra income, the quicker you'll reach your big financial goals.
- Becoming a lifelong learner and investing in your professional growth and development can help maximize your lifetime earnings.
- Increase your income further with multiple income streams, such as with passive income or other side hustle businesses.

## ACTION PLAN

In the companion *Her Money Rules! Financial Planner*, or your notebook, complete the following action steps:

- ▢ Determine if your current wage or salary is in line with your position, skills, and experience. For this step, you may need to do some market research. Look at current job listings for similar positions in similar fields. Consider your education and experience, and reflect on the value you bring to your current organization.
- ▢ If the answer is no for the prior step, consider asking for a raise. To prepare for the conversation, list your accomplishments over the past year and draft your pitch. Specifically, look for accomplishments that helped your organization cut costs and increase revenues, or accomplishments that improved productivity, efficiency, and customer service. When drafting your pitch, include the precise dollar amount you are requesting, the value you bring to the organization, and your recent accomplishments. Express your value and accomplishments as measurable benefits to the organization. Also, include future goals you're striving to achieve in your role that will benefit the organization.
- ▢ Create your professional growth and development plan. Use the Professional Growth & Development Plan in the companion *Her Money Rules! Financial Planner* or download and print additional copies at hermoneyrules.com/bonus. As you fill out your

professional growth and development plan, think about your career and what your career path goals are. Research and write your answers to these questions:

- What is the next promotion level in your organization or field?
- What qualifications and experience are required for that position?
- What certifications, degrees, training, or skills do you need to be best qualified?
- Make a list of the next steps you can take in your professional development to help you earn your next promotion.
- What books or training can you invest in to gain additional skills needed for that promotion?

☐ Besides optimizing the income at your current job, think about, research, and list other income ideas outside of that job. List at least ten side-hustle or other passive-income ideas. Choose the side hustle or passive income idea you'll pursue first.

## COMING UP IN RULE 6: BUILD YOUR EMERGENCY FUND

The next chapter covers the risks of going without an emergency fund and how to determine the right size for yours. You'll also learn how to use budgeting to reach your emergency fund goal.

# RULE 6

# BUILD YOUR EMERGENCY FUND

*"Save when you don't need it, and it'll be there for you when you do."*

*—Frank Sonnenberg*[1]

## CHRISTINE'S EMERGENCY

A few years ago, my niece Christine started having tooth pain. At first, over-the-counter pain medication helped, but the pain kept getting worse. The pain bothered her at work and kept her up at night.

Finally, Christine got an appointment to see her dentist and learned that she needed a root canal. The good news was that she had dental insurance. The bad news was that she was responsible for $500 of the total cost. This was bad news for Christine, because she was living paycheck to paycheck and didn't have $500. She was barely making enough money to cover her living expenses, and she didn't have an emergency fund.

Because the pain was too much to wait until she could save $500, she charged the amount on her credit card. This increased her credit card debt higher than she'd ever had before.

## RISKS OF NOT HAVING AN EMERGENCY FUND

Just like Christine, you may face emergencies in life that impact your finances. Thus, before paying off debt and investing to reach your big financial goal, I recommend you build your emergency fund. This is important because when the inevitable emergencies arise, you won't get sidetracked from fulfilling your other financial goals.

When we don't have emergency fund savings, how we pay for unexpected expenses could increase the total cost of that expense. When Christine used her credit card instead of savings to pay for her root canal treatment, the cost was higher. It took her eight months to pay off that debt, so her root canal cost her another $50 in interest. This increased the total cost from $500 to $550.

Not having an emergency fund can also cause financial stress and anxiety. When financial emergencies occur, you worry about how you're going to come up with the money. If you're already under financial strain, this can cause even more stress.

Not having an emergency fund is especially stressful if you're already living paycheck to paycheck. If you're living paycheck to paycheck, it's time to get out of that cycle, and having an emergency fund can help. Otherwise, you will continue to be someone with reasons why you can't build wealth.

## HOW BIG SHOULD YOUR EMERGENCY FUND BE?

Everyone's financial situation is unique. Therefore, the size of your emergency fund will depend on your financial situation, including your current earnings and living expenses.

If your income is low and you struggle to pay for basic living expenses, then I recommend building a $500 emergency fund. Once you've reached that goal, the next goal is to save at least one month's worth of living expenses and budget a *month ahead.* This strategy is sometimes called *using last month's paycheck for this month's bills*, as explained in Rule 4.

If your income is good and you're already budgeting a *month ahead*, I recommend building your emergency fund to cover one month's living expenses. Once you've reached that, shoot for saving three months' worth of living expenses.

Some financial experts recommend saving six months' worth of liquid cash savings. That amount will provide a good financial cushion in case of an unexpected job loss, business losses, or relocation. If your monthly living expenses are $2,000, you'd need a $12,000 emergency fund.

Whether you choose to save $500 or enough to cover several months of living expenses depends on how much financial risk you're willing to take. It also depends on how much you want to be self-insured, as discussed in Rule 3.

## HOW TO BUILD AN EMERGENCY FUND

Now that you've chosen your emergency fund savings goal, the next step is to make a plan for reaching that goal.

Begin by choosing a monthly savings target for your emergency fund. After that, revise your budget to incorporate this amount.

I recommend budgeting diligently until you reach your emergency fund savings goal. Be as frugal as you can and limit your spending to basic needs and essentials. Review Rule 3 for ideas on cutting expenses.

The quicker you reach your emergency fund goal, the sooner you'll gain peace of mind—and can focus on your other financial goals.

Start by saving at least 10 percent of your income. So, if your monthly income is $2,000, set a savings goal of $200 per month. Saving $200 a month might require trimming expenses in other parts of your budget, such as taking $50 each from groceries, clothing, entertainment, and dining out.

At the start of each month, or as soon as your paycheck arrives, transfer your budgeted amount straight into your emergency fund. Doing this early reduces the chance you'll spend that money on something else.

It's a good idea to open a savings account that's separate from the bank you use for your checking account. Even better, consider a high-yield savings or money market account, which typically earns more interest than a standard savings account.

Storing your emergency fund and other savings at a different bank helps you keep that money off limits. Since you won't see that money in your checking account, you're less likely to spend it.

Having your savings and checking accounts at the same bank makes it easy to transfer money within seconds, which can encourage impulsive spending. In contrast, keeping your savings at another bank creates a delay of three to five business days for transfers. This helps ensure you only use the money for what it's for—actual emergencies.

Once you've met your emergency fund savings goal, the next step is to pay off all your non-mortgage debt.

## KEY POINTS

- Not having an emergency fund puts you at financial risk and unnecessary stress.
- Have an emergency fund with at least $500 and up to six months' worth of living expenses, depending on your unique financial situation.
- Use budgeting to save as much as you can until you reach your emergency fund goal.
- The quicker you reach your emergency savings goal, the sooner you'll have peace of mind and can tackle your other financial goals.

## ACTION PLAN

In the companion *Her Money Rules! Financial Planner*, or your notebook, complete the following action steps:

- ☐ Choose and write your emergency fund savings goal as a dollar amount. I recommend a minimum of $500, or you can choose one to six months' worth of living expenses.
- ☐ To build your emergency fund, decide how much you'll budget and deposit into your savings account each month, then update next month's budget to reflect this.
- ☐ If you don't already have one, open a high-yield savings account and transfer your emergency fund savings there.

## COMING UP IN RULE 7: PAY OFF ALL YOUR NON-MORTGAGE DEBT

Accruing debt is a clear sign we're spending more than we earn and living beyond our means. In the next chapter, you'll learn strategies for paying off debt. You'll also understand whether using credit cards after becoming debt-free can be a useful financial tool for you, or something to avoid. You'll also learn the pros and cons of paying off mortgage debt early, and the pros and cons of renting versus owning your home.

# RULE 7

# PAY OFF ALL YOUR NON-MORTGAGE DEBT

*"Pay off debt ASAP, and not because it costs you money."*
*—Suze Orman*[1]

## MELISSA'S STORY OF STUDENT CREDIT CARD DEBT

In my first year of college in the mid-1990s, I recall seeing tables outside the student union promoting student credit cards. My friend Melissa and I each signed up for one of these credit cards.

I thought getting my first credit card was exciting and knew that building credit was important. The key was to make a purchase and then to make the monthly payments on time. Then the creditors would see me as someone worthy of giving more credit to.

This student credit card had a maximum balance of $250. You would think that these low balances would keep most college students out of trouble. For me, that was true in the beginning. I didn't accumulate significant credit card debt until graduate school.

By comparison, my friend Melissa found trouble right away. A mix of scholarships and savings from her parents covered her tuition, room, and board. However, Melissa found a part-time job to help cover her spending money.

By the middle of her first year, Melissa quit her part-time job because she was having trouble keeping up with her more challenging classes. After quitting her job, she started relying on her credit card more.

Soon Melissa had maxed out that first credit card. But because she always made the minimum payments on time each month, the bank rewarded her by doubling her credit line to $500. A year later, she had reached the new limit, but the bank wouldn't increase it again, so she applied for another credit card.

Melissa could make the small $10 to $25 minimum payments, and she planned to get a summer job to pay off the balances.

Yet, as time went on, both her credit card balances and the number of cards kept increasing. Melissa justified her spending. She figured once she graduated from college, she would land a good-paying job and could pay them off later. She resigned herself to the debt, and she kept spending. Melissa even splurged on a spring break trip to California.

At graduation, her credit card debt had grown to $10,000.

## THE PITFALLS OF DEBT

Debt can be useful in helping us get through periods of low income, such as during early adulthood. During emergencies or large unexpected expenses, debt can be especially useful. Debt can also provide a cushion to land on when we lose a job.

However, debt can easily become a source of trouble and a sign of trouble. Accruing debt shows we're spending more than we earn and living beyond our means.

Debt is the opposite of financial freedom because it creates a monthly liability that won't go away until fully paid off. Avoiding credit card debt helps you save money, lower stress, and preserve financial freedom.

Understanding the true cost of debt can be helpful. Let's say you charged $100 to your credit card three years ago for a bridesmaid dress. If you still haven't paid it off, your dress could now have a total cost of $170. This assumes a 20 percent average annual interest rate. It's possible this dress is also no longer in your wardrobe.

Here are some key reasons to avoid credit card and other consumer debt:

- **High Interest Rates**: Credit cards often have very high-interest rates, making it expensive to carry a balance. The average credit card interest rate as of publishing is 20 percent.
- **Debt Trap**: A debt trap is a situation where you take out more loans than you can afford, causing your debt to spiral out of control. This can happen when you continue to take out loans to pay off other debt, or when you borrow more to facilitate spending.
- **Negative Impact on Credit Score**: Carrying a high balance on your credit card can negatively affect your credit score. Having a bad credit score makes it harder to get loans or favorable interest rates in the future, such as home mortgage loans.
- **Financial Stress**: Debt can cause a lot of stress and anxiety, affecting your mental and emotional well-being. When your debt and monthly payments are

high, it can strain your finances by forcing you to prioritize debt payments over other financial needs.

- **Limits Future Financial Freedom**: Debt payments reduce the money you can save, invest, or put toward your goal of financial freedom.
- **Possible Fees and Penalties**: Missing payments or carrying a high balance can lead to additional fees and penalties, increasing your debt even further.

## MY STORY OF DEBT

Kent and I have been debt free, besides our mortgage debt, for about ten years. This has reduced our financial stress and helped us achieve financial freedom.

If we want to buy something, we pay for it with cash. If we can't afford to pay cash, we don't buy it.

However, throughout much of our working years, we accrued various debts. We had some credit card debt, a car loan, a medical loan, and a student loan. I share these scenarios below to show that sometimes debt can be useful or teach us lessons. Maybe you can learn from me, or take pride in being smarter than I was regarding debt.

### Credit Card Debt

I had $20,000 in credit card debt from my graduate school years. Looking back, that debt seemed inevitable and useful. Debt helped me during a time that I was 100 percent focused on investing in my education. However, this debt was also an overwhelming burden. I learned from this experience that I didn't want to be in credit card debt ever again. Since paying off that debt, I've diligently paid my credit card bill in full every month.

### Car Loan

Kent and I had a car loan for the only car we ever drove off the lot brand new. We paid the loan off in five years and had the car for another five years before we sold it. We ended up paying roughly $3,000 in interest over the five years of the loan. Since then, we've bought reliable, low-mileage used cars with cash up front.

### Medical Loan

We had a $5,000 medical loan, so my husband could correct low vision with artificial lenses. This was a no-interest loan, and we paid it off within eighteen months. No-interest loans can be helpful in paying for medical costs. However, it's critical to make each payment on time on these types of loans. If you don't, they could convert to a high-interest loan, even if you're late with only one payment. We made the payments on time, so we benefited from this no-interest loan.

### Student Loan

I had a student loan balance of roughly $20,000 after graduate school. I was fortunate to get a job that offered a 5 percent salary increase for employees with graduate degrees. That extra 5 percent in my paycheck was roughly the same amount as my monthly student loan payment. After making monthly payments for fourteen years, I made a lump sum payment and paid it off six years early.

## PAY OFF ALL NON-MORTGAGE DEBT BEFORE INVESTING

In Rule 6, I recommend you build up your emergency fund before paying off any credit card or other consumer debt. In this rule, Rule 7, I recommend paying off any consumer debt before you begin investing.

If you budget a significant chunk of money toward paying off debt each month, this will help you build the habit of budgeting for wealth creation. Once you pay off your debt, you can then redirect that money toward investing.

Another argument for paying off debt first is that a dollar paid toward debt will go further than the same dollar invested. That is because you'll save money on interest. And the money you save on debt interest will probably be more than you could earn by investing.

Credit card interest rates over the past ten years have averaged 12 to 22 percent. In comparison, the average annual return from a stock market index fund over the same period was 10 percent. Investing in rental property could provide an average return of 7 to 10 percent.

Let's say you have $1,000. You can choose either to pay off credit card debt or to invest it in the stock market. If you pay off the credit card debt, you'll save 20 percent in interest. If you invest it instead, you might make an average return of 10 percent per year. Thus, paying off the debt could result in a 10 percent difference or $100 savings after one year.

## A COUNTERARGUMENT: PAY OFF DEBT AND INVEST AT THE SAME TIME

Not all financial experts agree that you should pay off debt before investing. Instead, they suggest people invest right away, even while building an emergency fund or paying off debt. Their argument is that, for some people, it may take years or even decades to pay off debt and save enough before they feel ready to invest.[2]

Some people may see money in a savings account and spend it, creating a cycle. They build up their savings and spend it. Then they build up their savings and spend them again. Therefore, they may never feel they have enough savings to start investing. Yet, if they put extra money into an investment account instead of a savings account, they may feel less tempted to spend it.

Some financial experts argue that to build wealth, you need to start investing now, even if it's just a small portion of your income.[3] I understand their perspective and agree that, for some people, this approach makes sense. Ultimately, based on your unique financial situation, beliefs, and habits, you can decide what's best for you.

## STRATEGIES FOR PAYING OFF YOUR DEBT

I've covered the reasons to avoid non-mortgage debt and why it's important to pay off this debt as soon as you can. Now, it's time to cover strategies for paying off your debt.

If you built your emergency fund by cutting expenses or increasing your income, you can now use that money to pay down debt.

If you have multiple debts, there are several payoff strategies to choose from.

## Avalanche versus Snowball

One strategy for paying off debt is tackling the highest-interest balance first. This strategy, called the Avalanche Method, will save you the most in debt interest as you pay down the debt.

Another strategy is to focus on paying off the smallest debt first. This is called the Snowball Method and helps build momentum as you eliminate each balance.

Let's look at these two strategies using an example. Let's say you have the following debts:

- Visa card at 20.2 percent interest with a balance of $5,450
- Mastercard at 13.2 percent interest with a balance of $2,230
- Car loan at 7.1 percent with a balance of $7,110

With the Avalanche Method, you would put as much money as possible toward the Visa card, since it carries the highest interest rate. Continue to make the minimum payments on the Mastercard and the car loan. After paying off the Visa balance, you would then move on to paying down the Mastercard debt.

Using the Snowball Method of paying off the smallest balance first, you begin by putting as much money as possible toward paying off the Mastercard. Again, continue making the minimum payments on the other two debts. Once you pay off the Mastercard, you shift your focus to the Visa card.

You'll see progress more quickly by paying off the smallest balance first, regardless of interest rate. In this example, you can eliminate the lowest balance faster than the highest-interest debt. This early win can motivate you, boost your confidence, and give you a sense of accomplishment to keep going. You may even feel inspired to tighten your spending further so you can pay down the next debt more aggressively.

### Consolidate Your Credit Card Debt

Another strategy for paying off debt is to consolidate or merge your debt. This strategy is mainly for credit card debt. Consolidating your debt simplifies your repayment by combining multiple balances into one loan. Depending on your credit score and the type of consolidation you use, you may get a lower interest rate. In that case, more of what you pay goes directly toward reducing your balance instead of interest charges.

There are four common ways to consolidate credit card debt: balance transfer, personal loan, home equity loan or line of credit, or refinancing your mortgage.

#### 1. Balance Transfer:

The balance transfer option is where you move your high-interest credit card balances to a new credit card with a lower interest rate. The key is to avoid using the new credit card for any additional purchases.

This option is best if you can qualify for a balance transfer with a 0 percent promotional interest rate. This allows you to pay off your debt without accumulating more interest during the promotional period, usually six to twenty-one months.

Watch out for balance transfer fees and the interest rate that kicks in after the promotional period ends. However, if the fee and ongoing interest are still lower than your current credit card's rates, a balance transfer could be a smart choice.

### 2. Personal Loan:

With this option, you take out a personal loan with a lower interest rate than your credit cards. You then use the loan to pay off your credit card debt. You'll repay the loan in fixed monthly installments over a set period. Personal loans may have origination fees, and the interest rate will depend on your credit score.

### 3. Home Equity Loan or Line of Credit:

Another option is to use the equity in your home to secure a loan with a lower interest rate. You then use that new loan to pay off your credit card debt.

Similar to a personal loan, you would repay the home equity loan in fixed monthly installments over a set period. Keep in mind, if you don't make the monthly payments on a home equity loan or line of credit, you risk losing your home to foreclosure.

### 4. Refinance Your Home Mortgage:

Refinancing your home into a new mortgage to pay off consumer debt is my least recommended option. Refinancing a mortgage often comes with high fees. This option also has a longer repayment period for that debt. If you roll your credit card debt onto a new 30-year mortgage, you'll be paying for that debt over thirty years. You'll also end up paying more interest over the long term.

Using your home's equity to pay off consumer debt can also be risky. If you fall behind on your mortgage payments, you could lose your home to foreclosure.

## THE CREDIT CARD DEBATE

Once you've chosen your debt repayment strategy, it's time to decide if credit cards are going to be a good financial tool for you moving forward.

If you're familiar with Dave Ramsey, you probably know he recommends cutting up all credit cards and never using them for any reason.[4]

My stance is that if you have a spending problem or worry you'll get into debt trouble again, then don't have credit cards.

However, if used wisely, credit cards can be a helpful tool for managing your money. This means only using them for purchases you already have the money for and paying the balance in full each month. It's also important to create your perfect budget each month using last month's income.

I charge most of my monthly expenses to one credit card because then I only have one bill to pay each month. The other benefit of using my credit card is that I accumulate airline miles that Kent and I use for travel.

You'll need to decide for yourself whether using credit cards is a benefit for you, or if they'll only get you into debt trouble.

If you decide to use credit, I recommend using only one credit card. Put the others in a safe place or cut them up. Then, use this one credit card only for expenses you have already budgeted, and the money to pay for those expenses is already in the bank. Ultimately, as discussed above, it's important to stop accruing debt.

If using credit cards ever becomes a problem, then it's time to do what Dave Ramsey advises and cut them up.

## THE MORTGAGE DEBT VS RENTING DEBATE

This rule, Rule 7, is to pay off all your non-mortgage debt. There are some financial experts who believe that mortgage debt is not as bad as other debts, like consumer debt.[5]

These experts also believe that buying a home with the help of a mortgage is a smart way to build wealth. Each month, you increase your ownership, or equity, by paying down the mortgage.

Your equity also grows as your home's value rises. The average home value has increased by 3.8 percent per year over the past thirty years.

Other financial experts argue you can build wealth faster by renting instead of buying a home with a mortgage. The experts say you could invest the money instead of spending it on buying and maintaining a home. Investing this money can earn returns, which you can reinvest to grow your wealth over time.[6]

A home you own can also be a liability. Homeownership comes with many ongoing costs, such as mortgage interest, insurance, property taxes, and maintenance. Maintenance can include things like landscaping, painting, roof and gutter cleaning, pest control, and furnace tune-ups. As a renter, your landlord covers these expenses.

Another financial benefit of renting your home instead of owning it is that you know exactly what you'll pay for housing each month. You won't have the regular and unexpected maintenance or repair costs that come with owning a home.

I can see both the advantages and disadvantages of renting versus owning your home. It's a choice you'll need to consider, and your decision may depend on your values and lifestyle.

If you own your own home with a mortgage and want to reach your financial goals faster, consider renting out your home to someone else. You can then move into a rental that meets your needs and fits your budget.

## THE PAYING OFF YOUR MORTGAGE EARLY DEBATE

I'd like to share another debate among financial experts, which is whether to pay off your mortgage debt early.[7]

There are pros and cons to paying off your mortgage early, but the numbers don't lie. Mortgage and investment calculators show that investing extra money builds more long-term wealth than using it to pay down your mortgage.

Let's say you owe $200,000 on your mortgage at 7 percent interest, and you have ten years of monthly payments remaining. Let's also assume you received a $200,000 inheritance from your wealthy and generous grandparents.

One option would be to use that inheritance to pay off your $200,000 mortgage now. This option would save you $78,660 in interest that you would've paid over the remaining ten years of the loan.

An alternative option would be to invest that $200,000 in the stock market instead of paying off your mortgage. With a 10 percent average annual return, in ten years you would have $543,580, more than double your investment. With this option, you would be $464,920 wealthier after ten years than if you'd used the money to pay off your mortgage.

Let's consider the first option further. Let's say you paid off your mortgage with the $200,000 inheritance *and* invested what your monthly mortgage payment would have been for ten years. Assuming a monthly mortgage payment of $2,322 and a 10 percent average annual return, your investment balance after ten years would be $480,740. In that case, your wealth would still be about $62,840 lower than if you had invested that $200,000 as a lump sum.

You can test this out for yourself. If you have a mortgage, you can use a mortgage calculator like mortgagecalculator.org.[8] Use the calculator to see how much faster you could pay off your mortgage by adding extra money each month toward the principal. Then use an investment calculator, like the one at calculator.net, to compare how much your money might grow through investing versus paying off your mortgage early.

## KEY POINTS

- Accruing debt is a sign that we're spending more than we earn and living beyond our means.
- Debt gets in our way of achieving financial freedom because it becomes a monthly expense that won't go away until it's paid off.
- Strategies for paying off debt include paying off the highest interest debt first or paying off the smallest size debt first.

- Another strategy is to consolidate your debt to simplify your repayment and lower the interest rate.

## ACTION PLAN

In the companion *Her Money Rules! Financial Planner*, or your notebook, complete the following action steps:

- ☐ Choose your debt pay-off strategy: 1) Use the Snowball Method of paying off the smallest sized debt first; 2) Use the Avalanche Method of paying off the highest interest debt first; or 3) Consolidate your debt into one debt account with one monthly payment.
- ☐ List all your current non-mortgage debt. Then place a number ranking next to each one, reflecting your debt payoff strategy and the order you will pay off your debt.
- ☐ For the debt you plan to pay off first, decide and write how much per month you will pay down that debt. Then update next month's budget to reflect this.

## COMING UP IN RULE 8: CHOOSE YOUR INVESTMENT STRATEGY

In the next chapter, you'll learn the two best investment strategies for building wealth. You'll learn how using annual return on investment calculations can help you choose the best investments. You'll also get detailed steps for implementing the investment strategy you choose.

# RULE 8

# CHOOSE YOUR INVESTMENT STRATEGY

*"Being rich is having money; being wealthy is having time."*
*—Margaret Bonanno*[1]

## LET YOUR MONEY WORK FOR YOU

After you've built an emergency fund and paid off all non-mortgage debt, you're ready to start investing. You can now use the money you were putting toward emergency fund savings or debt payments and invest it instead.

If you're still working on building your emergency fund or paying off debt, you could wait to invest. Or you could decide to begin investing some of your income now.

In Rule 2, you created your big financial goal and turned that into a dollar goal. If your big financial goal is to build wealth, then your initial investment goal might be to grow your first $100,000. Because once you've reached your first $100,000, you can then let that money work for you.

For example, in the stock market, your invested money can work for you and grow through compounding. Investment compounding is when your money grows not only on the original amount you invested but also on the returns you've already earned. In simple terms, it's like earning interest on your interest. Over time, this snowball effect helps your money build faster, because each year your gains generate more gains. The longer you leave your investment to grow, the more powerful compounding becomes.

With compounding, a stock market investment could double every 7.2 years on average. This assumes an average rate of return of 10 percent per year.[2] Rate of return is the percentage gain or loss on an investment over a specific period and can include returns from interest, dividends, or share price changes.

You can use the Rule of 72 to calculate how many years it would take to double your investment by dividing 72 by the annual rate of return. I worked out the numbers for you, up to 14% annually, in Figure 1 below.

### Figure 1. Number of Years to Double an Investment Using the Rule of 72

| Rate of Return | Years | Rate of Return | Years |
|---|---|---|---|
| 1% | 72 | 8% | 9 |
| 2% | 36 | 9% | 8 |
| 3% | 24 | 10% | 7.2 |
| 4% | 18 | 11% | 6.5 |
| 5% | 14.4 | 12% | 6 |
| 6% | 12 | 13% | 5.5 |
| 7% | 10.3 | 14% | 5.1 |

Assuming an annual average rate of return of 10 percent, even if you didn't invest another dollar, your original $100,000 could grow to $800,000 in approximately 22 years. Yet if you continued to invest additional dollars, let's say $500 per month, you could grow $100,000 into almost $1.3 million in that same period. See Figures 2 and 3 below.

**Figure 2. Compounding Growth of $100,000 by Year at 10 Percent Average Annual Rate of Return**

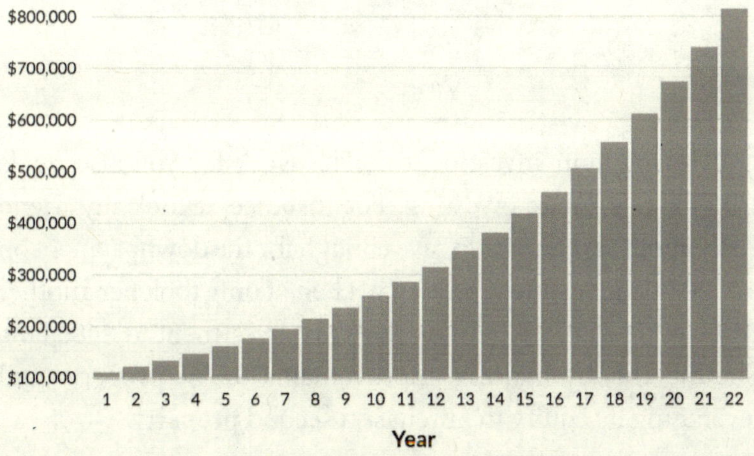

## Figure 3. Compounding Growth of $100,000 by Year at 10 Percent Average Annual Rate of Return vs. Investing an Additional $500 per Month

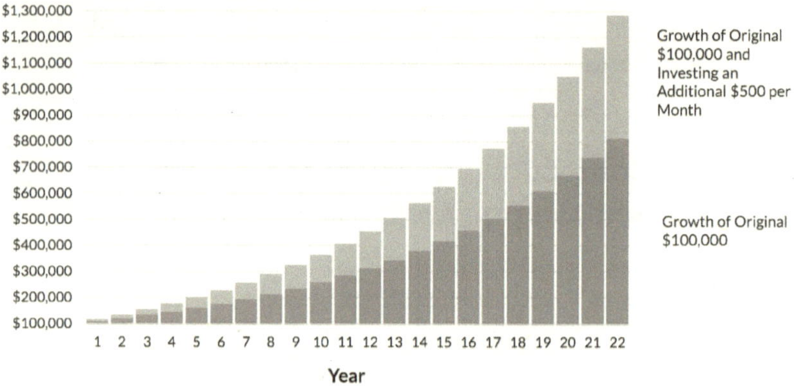


Having your investment dollars work for you also holds true for real estate investing. For instance, it took my friend Kelly about seven years to save enough for the downpayment on a $220,000 investment property. Then, it only took her another three years to more than double this investment to $480,000. She did this by making improvements to the property and leveraging its equity to purchase a second property.

Regardless of your dollar goal, it's time to choose your investment strategy.

There are many things you can invest your money in, but this chapter focuses on two major investments:

- Option 1: Invest in the stock market
- Option 2: Invest in real estate

Other investment options include investing in a business, cryptocurrency, options, bonds, commodities, money markets, and certificates of deposit. All investment options have varying levels of risk and return. So please do your research when deciding on your investment strategy.

I recommend the stock market and real estate strategies because I believe they are the two best ways to build wealth. You can choose one or the other, or you can invest in both. You could even use investing in the stock market to save up enough to invest in a real estate property.

## OPTION 1: INVEST IN THE STOCK MARKET

### Rich, the Fearless Stock Market Investor

A relative of mine, Rich, has been investing in the stock market since he was fourteen years old.

His grandfather was in the mutual fund business. When Rich was ten years old, his grandfather gave him a tour of his office and shared the basics of investing.

A few years later, Rich made his first investment. He put $300 he earned from mowing lawns into a mutual fund. He remembers checking the newspaper every day to see how his mutual fund was doing.

After Rich completed college and got married, he invested a portion of his income each month. He created a big financial goal—to earn as much from his investments as he earned from his job, and he met that goal when he was fifty-six years old.

I call Rich the fearless stock market investor because he doesn't panic whenever there's a downturn in the overall stock market or economy. He stays the course and sticks to his strategy.

In his sixty years of investing, Rich has seen many downturns in the stock market and just as many upswings. He saw the stock market crash of 1987, the dotcom bubble of 2001, and the 2008 crash triggered by the Financial Crisis. He also experienced the 2020 crash following the outbreak of COVID-19. After each of these downturns, the stock market recovered and kept growing.

Also, as I write this in early October 2025, the U.S. Stock Market hit an all-time high. This occurred after the market recovered all its losses from the April 2025 crash following U.S. trade policy decisions.

In Rich's experience, the stock market always goes up. It has its ups and downs, but over time, the average value keeps going up. See Figure 4 below.

Understanding that the stock market always goes up, Rich took out a second mortgage on his home back in 1982. This was a $20,000 mortgage, and he invested all of it in the stock market. In early 1982, the Dow Jones Industrial Average Index had dropped to a low of 824. In October 2025, the Index reached an all-time high of just over 46,700.[3] That averages out to a 9.7 percent a year gain in the 44-year period between 1982 and 2025. That would mean that Rich's $20,000 investment in 1982 could now be worth roughly $1.3 million.

The biggest lessons I learned from Rich:

- Over time, the value of the stock market always goes up.
- Whether the stock market has a correction or crash, you still own the same number of shares as you did before.

- Like any investment or business deal, the general strategy is to buy low and sell high.
- Take a long-term approach to stock market investing.

**Figure 4. Cumulative Percent Returns of Dow Jones vs. S&P 500 Index 1980 to 2024**[4]

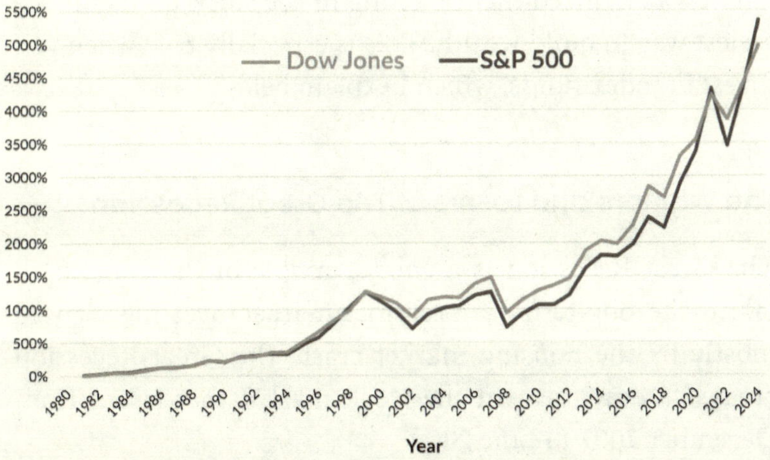


## You Too Can Be a Fearless Stock Market Investor

Like Rich, you can also be a fearless stock market investor. Don't let fear dictate your investment decisions. Instead, let your research inform your decisions and then stick to your plan.

Historically, the stock market has been full of corrections and crashes. If you are someone who lets fear drive your decisions when the inevitable downturns happen, then stock market investing might not be for you. The worst thing you can do is cash out your investments when there is a decline. This is selling low instead of selling high.

Many people get into the stock market when things are going well and values are rising. But when a correction happens, they decide it's not for them and pull their money out.

You'll increase your chances of success if you take a long-term approach like Rich. Staying invested is the key to long-term growth. After researching the material for this book, I'm now convinced that investing in the stock market is the easiest way to build wealth. This is especially true when you invest in index funds, which I explain below.

### The Winners and Losers of The Great Recession

The Great Recession is a good example of the benefits of taking the long-term view on stock market investing. Caused mostly by the housing market crash, the Great Recession created a downturn in the stock market that lasted from December 2007 to June 2009.[5]

Those who had investments in the stock market prior to the recession became either winners or losers, depending on the decisions they made.

Individuals who kept their stock investments during and after the recession grew their wealth. Those who got out of the stock market potentially saw their wealth cut in half.

The stock market as a whole fell in value during the Great Recession by about 50 percent. The S&P 500 fell by over 50 percent at its lowest point.[6] Thus, those who sold could have lost as much as 50 percent of their wealth. Actual losses would have depended on the collection of stocks they owned. After the stock market fell, it took between four and six years to get back to pre-recession levels.

However, in the ten years between 2009 and 2019, the stock market increased by 330 percent.[7] As a result, those who kept their investment shares recovered their losses and saw their investments continue to grow.

Let's assume someone had $100,000 invested in an index fund that represented the total U.S. stock market just prior to the Great Recession. If that person had stayed invested through the recession and for the ten years that followed, their original $100,000 would have grown to about $220,000 by the end of 2019.

If this same person also invested $10,000 a year during those ten years, their total investment could have grown to around $450,000 by 2019. These calculations are based on the S&P 500 average annual rate of return of 17.8 percent over that 10-year period.[8]

The Great Recession offers valuable lessons for future downturns. Don't panic and don't sell. Stay invested and wait for the likely recovery. Even better, keep investing as much as you can while stock prices are low.

## Stock Market Definitions

Before diving into what I believe are the best stock market investment strategies, below are some common stock market investment terms and definitions.

### *Stock Market*

The U.S. stock market is where investors and traders buy and sell stocks, which are shares of companies and other financial instruments.

Most stocks are bought and sold, or traded, electronically through stock exchanges. The two main stock exchanges in the United States are the New York Stock Exchange and the National Association of Securities Dealers, also known as Nasdaq.

### *Bear Market versus Bull Market*

A bear market is when average stock prices are in decline for a period and can show a weakening economy. A bull market is when stock prices are on the rise and show a favorable economy.

Market downturns during a bear market are unavoidable and happen regularly. Understanding the reality that bear and bull markets happen can help ease your fears. Remember, the market has always trended upward over time.

### *Individual Stocks*

Individual stocks make up the stock market. When you buy a share of stock, you become a shareholder. It's like owning a small piece or share of a company.

Normally, the value of a stock goes up and down depending on how well the company is doing. If a company is earning strong profits and meeting expectations, its stock value typically goes up. If the company isn't doing well, the value of its stock usually goes down.

### *Returns and Dividends*

When you invest in stocks, you can earn returns and dividends.

In simple terms, a return is how much you have gained or lost from your investment in the stock. Let's say you bought a share of stock at $30 a share. A year later, if that stock value is $35, then your return on that investment is $5 or 16.7 percent.

Some stocks pay dividends, which are regular income payments from the companies you own shares in. The amount of the dividend can vary and depends on the profits of the company. The company determines the percentage of its profits to be used for dividends. You can choose to reinvest your dividend earnings into more shares of stock or receive them as cash.

A total return on a stock investment includes the increase in share price of the stock and the value of any dividends received.

### *Market Indexes*

A market index is a representation of the overall stock market. Investors use indexes as a benchmark to understand how the stock market is performing overall. If the index goes up on average, the prices of the stocks in the market are going up. If the index goes down on average, the prices are going down. The Dow Jones Industrial Average, S&P 500, and Nasdaq Composite are the three main U.S. market indexes.

- **Dow Jones Industrial Average**: Also known as the Dow or Dow Jones, this is a U.S. stock market index that includes thirty large companies. Unlike other indexes, the Dow is not based on the size of the companies. Instead, it's based on their share prices. There are always thirty companies in the index, but the index sometimes changes the list of companies it includes.

- **Standard and Poor's 500**: Mainly known as the S&P 500, this index tracks the stock performance of 500 of the largest companies listed on U.S. stock exchanges. The index includes approximately 80 percent of the total market value of U.S. public companies.
- **Nasdaq Composite**: This index includes almost all stocks listed on the Nasdaq or the National Association of Securities Dealers stock exchange. Similar to the S&P 500, the Nasdaq Composite Index is also based on the market value of the companies included in its index.

### *Bonds*

Although I primarily write about stocks and the stock market in this section, I'll briefly touch on bonds. Like stocks, bonds are a common investment option and are frequently part of investment funds, as discussed below.

A bond is like a loan that you, the bondholder, give to a government, municipality, or corporation. As the bondholder, you'll receive regular interest payments. When the bond reaches its maturity date, the bond issuer will pay you back the original amount you loaned, called the principal. The issuer also promises to pay you interest throughout the bond's term.

### *Investment Funds*

The average investor doesn't invest in individual stocks or bonds. Instead, they invest in an investment fund, which is a collection of stocks, bonds, or a mix of both. The most common types of investment funds are mutual funds, index funds, and exchange-traded funds, also called ETFs.

- **Mutual Funds:** A mutual fund pools money from many people to buy a diverse mix of stocks, bonds, or other investments. Each investor owns shares in the fund. The value of a mutual fund share is determined at the end of each trading day.
- **ETFs:** An exchange-traded fund or ETF is an investment that works like a mutual fund but trades on stock exchanges like a regular stock. ETFs can be bought and sold throughout the day at market prices, making them flexible and easy to trade.
- **Index Funds:** An index fund is a type of mutual fund or ETF designed to match the performance of a specific market index, like the S&P 500. Therefore, index funds invest in the stocks of companies that are included in the index.

## Examples of Annual Return on Investment Calculations

To help you compare and choose among various stock investments, I've included annual return on investment calculations. They also show how your money can grow in the stock market.

### *Simple Annual Return on Investment Calculation Based on Share Price Only*

This annual return on investment calculation uses a simple calculation based on share price only. To get the annual return on investment in dollars, you subtract the starting value from the ending value. If the number is positive, your investment gained in value. If the number is negative, you have an investment loss. Here's the annual return on investment formula:

*Annual return on investment = ending value - starting value*

To get the percent annual return on investment, divide the annual return on investment amount by the starting value, then multiply that by 100. Here's the percent annual return on investment formula:

*Percent annual return on investment = (annual return on investment ÷ starting value) x 100*

To illustrate, let's say you purchased $1,400 of Johnson & Johnson stock in January 2023, with stock symbol JNJ. The stock price was $140 per share, giving you ten shares. Thus, the *starting value* of your investment was *$1,400.* In December 2023, the stock price was $150 per share. Multiplying $150 by ten shares, the *ending value* of your investment was *$1,500.* This gave you a total annual return of $100. Note, this example is not based on actual JNJ stock results.

For this example, the annual return on investment calculation is:

*$1,500 ending value - $1,400 starting value = $100 annual return on investment*

The percent annual return on investment calculation for this example is:

*($100 annual return on investment ÷ $1,400 starting value) x 100 = 7.1 percent annual return on investment*

Based on these two calculations, your annual return on investment in JNJ stocks was $100 and your percent annual return on investment was 7.1.

### *Total Annual Return on Investment Calculation Based on Share Price and Dividend Earnings*

To include dividend earnings in the annual return on investment calculation, you add the dividend earnings to the ending value of your investment to get the total ending value.

Using the above example again, let's assume JNJ paid you $1 per share per quarter in 2023, or $4 per share annually for all of 2023. Multiplying the ten shares by the $4 dividend gives you $40 in *total dividend payments.*

To calculate the total annual return on investment, you add the $40 dividend to your investment's *annual return* of $100 to get $140.

Here's the total annual return on investment formula:

*Total annual return on investment = (ending value + total dividend payments) - starting value*

Using the JNJ example, the total annual return on investment calculation is:

*($1,500 ending value + $40 total dividend payments) - $1,400 starting value = $140 total annual return on investment*

Next, to get the percent total annual return on investment, use this calculation:

*Percent total annual return on investment = (total annual return on investment ÷ starting value) x 100*

The percent total annual return on investment calculation for the JNJ example is:

*($140 total annual return on investment ÷ $1,400 starting value) x 100 = 10 percent total annual return on investment*

Thus, including the dividend payments, the total annual return on your investment was 10 percent.

## Stock Market Investment Strategies

This section includes four of the most common stock market investment strategies: index funds, non-index mutual funds, target retirement funds, and buying and selling individual stocks.

### *A. Index Funds*

Of all stock market investment strategies, index funds are among the most popular and widely recommended by financial experts. They also typically have lower fees than actively managed mutual funds.

As mentioned above, an index fund is a collection or portfolio of stocks and bonds that mimics a stock market index. If an index fund is based on the S&P 500, for example, the fund manager will include stocks from all 500 companies tracked by the index.

John Bogle, founder of Vanguard, created the first publicly available index fund in 1976.[9] However, index funds have only recently become popular and recommended by financial experts.

Index funds are a preferred investment because they have a wide range of stocks, lower risk, and greater diversification. They also can be a great tool for long-term investment growth because of their historical performance. In addition, index funds can save you time compared to selecting and managing individual stocks yourself.

### *B. Non-Index Mutual Funds*

Before index funds became popular, traditional mutual funds were the most common investment. Actively managed mutual funds are also called non-index mutual funds.

The major difference is that fund managers passively manage index funds, whereas they actively manage non-index mutual funds.

While index fund managers try to match market performance, non-index mutual fund managers attempt to outperform the market.

Non-index mutual funds typically have higher fees than index funds, which can eat into your overall returns. These higher costs stem from the time and effort required to manage these mutual funds actively, along with the added expenses from more frequent buying and selling.

Interestingly, actively managed non-index mutual funds can outperform index funds over the short term, but often underperform over the long-term.[10]

Some investment experts advise against trying to beat the market. Yet many fund managers and individual investors still try.

### *C. Target Retirement Funds*

Another mutual fund investment strategy is to invest in target retirement funds. These funds are also called target date funds or lifecycle funds. The fund's name usually includes a year, representing the year the investor plans to retire, such as *Target Retirement 2040.*

A target retirement fund invests in a mix of stocks, bonds, and short-term reserves. Short-term reserves are investments in interest-bearing bank deposits, money market instruments, U.S. Treasury bills, and short-term bonds.

Similar to other non-index mutual funds, target retirement funds are actively managed. Target retirement funds take more investment risks when you're young and gradually shift to more conservative investments as you approach retirement. When an investor has decades before retirement, the fund has a higher proportion of stocks. As your retirement date gets closer, the fund has a higher proportion of bonds and short-term reserves.

Investors can choose a target retirement fund closest to their planned retirement date. Once selected, you simply let the investment grow until you retire.

Like other non-index mutual funds, these funds are more costly to manage. As a result, they charge higher fees to investors compared to index funds.

### *D. Buying and Selling Individual Stocks*

Buying and selling individual stocks and creating your own investment portfolio is another investment strategy. This is the highest-risk option, whether you're knowledgeable about individual stock investing or not.

Some people find investing in individual stocks to be worthwhile. You have complete control over which companies you invest in. There is also the potential for high returns if you're successful in picking high-performing stocks. You also know exactly where you invest your money, and you avoid the management fees associated with managed mutual funds.

However, investing in individual stocks also comes with drawbacks. Individual stocks can be very volatile and risky, exposing you to higher risk. Managing a portfolio of individual stocks is time-consuming because it requires significant research and active management. This approach can also result in a less diversified portfolio, increasing your vulnerability to market fluctuations. You also risk making emotional investment decisions based on market swings, which can negatively affect your returns.

## How to Implement Your Stock Investment Strategy

As mentioned above, investing in index funds, including total market and S&P 500 index funds, is a widely recommended strategy for both new and experienced investors. It's also my preferred strategy for long-term growth.

Regardless of your stock market investment strategy, this section will help you implement that strategy in three steps: 1) open an online investment account, 2) add money to your investment account, and 3) invest the money.

If you choose to invest in real estate instead, you can skip this section. However, if you need time to save enough cash for your first real estate investment, you can grow this money by investing in the stock market.

Also, if your employer offers a matching program with your 401(k) or retirement plan, be sure to take advantage of it. Your employer will match your contributions dollar for dollar up to a certain percentage of your income, usually between 3 and 5 percent. For example, if the match is 3 percent, contribute at least that much to get the full employer match. This is essentially free money.

### *1. Open an Online Investment Account*

Depending on your financial goals, you can open a Roth IRA, a taxable investment account, or both. If your employer offers one, you could also contribute to a workplace retirement account.

A Roth IRA, or Roth Individual Retirement Account, is a retirement savings account that allows you to contribute after-tax income and grow your investments tax-free. Unlike a traditional IRA, withdrawals in retirement are tax free as long as you meet two primary conditions:

1) The account must have been open for at least five years; and
2) You must be at least fifty-nine and a half years old when you take withdrawals.

There are also no required minimum distributions with a ROTH IRA, so you can withdraw as much or as little as you want.

If your big financial goal is to retire early or achieve financial freedom before age fifty-nine and a half, a taxable investment account is one option. Or you could invest in both a Roth IRA and a taxable account. This way, you can use the earnings from your taxable investment account to cover expenses until you reach fifty-nine and a half. Once you've reached that age, you can begin withdrawing earnings from your Roth IRA penalty and tax-free.

You might also choose a taxable investment account if you plan on using your investment money to fund some other big financial goal before you reach fifty-nine and a half.

Otherwise, a Roth IRA is best if you plan to retire at or after fifty-nine and a half.

If you have money left after maxing out your Roth IRA contributions, that provides another reason to open a taxable investment account and invest the extra funds there.

Keep in mind that using a taxable investment account can make your taxes more complicated. Investment income, capital gains, dividends, and interest earned from your taxable investment account are subject to annual taxes.

Whether you open a Roth IRA or a taxable investment account, I recommend choosing a low-cost investment provider. Based on my research, three commonly used low-cost financial service companies are Schwab, Vanguard, and Fidelity. These providers have minimal management fees and won't charge you commissions on your contributions.

### *2. Add Money to Your Investment Account*

Once you've opened your retirement or investment account, it's time to add money to it. Maybe you have a chunk of money you've been growing in a savings account. You can now transfer that to your investment account.

You'll also want to build a monthly investment amount into your budget. Having met your emergency fund and debt reduction goals, redirect those dollars to your investment budget.

For a Roth IRA, for 2025, you can contribute up to $7,000 per year if you're younger than fifty. If you're fifty and older, you can contribute up to $8,000 per year.[11]

If you have a lump sum to invest from your savings, you can first max out your contributions to your Roth IRA for the year. Then put the rest into a taxable investment account. Or you can invest the entire amount in your taxable investment account.

### *3. Invest the Money*

Usually, when you first open a retirement or investment account and add money, that money will sit in a cash account. The next step is to choose the investment funds you want and decide how much or what percentage of your money to put into each one.

You'll want to choose one or more index funds, actively managed funds, or a target retirement fund. Instead, and against my best advice, you could invest in individual stocks.

Each month, you can put your investment contribution into one fund or split it by amount or percentage across several funds.

For example, let's say you have $5,000 ready to transfer to your newly created investment account. You could decide to put 50 percent in a total market index fund and the other 50 percent in an S&P 500 index fund. Then, you could allocate $500 each month in the future, which you decide to split equally between the two funds.

During my research, these index funds were frequently recommended by financial experts and are offered by Fidelity, Schwab, and Vanguard, respectively:

FSKAX Fidelity Total Market Index Fund
FXAIX Fidelity 500 Index Fund
FZROX Fidelity Zero Total Market Index Fund
SWPPX Schwab S&P 500 Index Fund
SWTSX Schwab Total Stock Market Index Fund
VFIAX Vanguard 500 Index Admiral Shares
VTSAX Vanguard Total Stock Market Admiral Shares

Once you've decided on an index fund, decide which version of the index to invest in: the ETF or the mutual fund. As defined earlier, an ETF is an exchange-traded fund and trades like a regular stock. Funds tracking specific indexes often have both types.

If you're investing within a retirement account like a Roth IRA, you'll want to choose the mutual fund type. If you're investing within a taxable investment account, the ETF version is preferable because of the tax implications. In short, ETFs are structured to avoid distributing capital gains as often, and you pay taxes only when you sell your shares and realize a gain.

## OPTION 2: INVEST IN REAL ESTATE

### Jerry's Small Real Estate Empire

Five years before I became a landlord myself, I rented a cute little 1940s house with two other roommates. My landlord was Jerry, who owned and managed four rental houses. I learned that managing and maintaining these rentals was his only job.

Jerry's lifestyle inspired me, and I loved talking with him about his rentals. Learning Jerry's story and observing how he ran his rental business planted a seed in my mind. For the first time, I saw the potential of being a landlord myself.

Jerry shared with me that the house I rented was his first rental. In the early 1990s, he purchased his first property with a down payment of $12,000. He qualified for the mortgage with three months of paystubs from a seasonal job.

After purchasing his first rental property and making improvements to it, he bought a second one. He used equity from the first property as the down payment. He also used his rental income from the first property to qualify for the second mortgage.

Jerry continued to buy additional rental properties until he had nine single-family homes. He used the existing equity of his previous rentals as down payments for each new house. As the number of rentals grew, his rental income and net worth grew. It wouldn't surprise me if his net worth is now well over $2 million, thirty years after he purchased his first rental property.

## Real Estate Investment Strategies

There are different strategies for investing in real estate. You can invest in single-family homes, multifamily homes, commercial property, and storage units.

You can be a solo investor and own these investments yourself, or you can join a partnership with other investors.

Alternatively, you can invest in Real Estate Investment Trusts also known as REITs. Below, I go into more detail on solo investing and REITs, including how to manage risk and example return on investment calculations.

### A. Solo Investing

As a solo investor, you own and manage your real estate properties as a personal business. This strategy doesn't prevent you from hiring a property management company that can manage your tenants, rent collection, and property maintenance. However, your rental business will be more profitable if you manage it yourself.

#### *Managing Risk*

Owning real estate can be a good way to earn income and build wealth. However, as with any investment, there are risks. You can manage risk by doing your homework, treating your rental property as a business, and being smart about how you manage your rental.

Learn as much as you can about state and local landlord-tenant laws. Also, learn the common and proven practices of being a landlord. Below are a few proven practices to keep your risks low and help you decide if being a landlord is for you.

Landlord proven practices:

- **Provide Excellent Customer Service:** Keep communication open and respond promptly to tenant concerns and maintenance requests. Also, respect tenants' privacy by giving proper notice before entering the rental property.
- **Know the Laws:** Research and stay updated on your state and local landlord-tenant laws to avoid legal issues.
- **Screen Tenants Thoroughly:** Do background checks, screen for credit risk, verify income, and check references to ensure reliable tenants.
- **Clear Lease Agreements:** Ensure lease agreements are comprehensive, follow landlord-tenant laws, and cover all expectations and policies.
- **Keep Records:** Maintain detailed records of all communications, repairs, and transactions.
- **Don't Be a Wimpy Landlord:** For any and every lease agreement violation, document those violations and send notices. Don't lose your rights as a landlord by allowing tenants to violate the terms of their rental agreement.[12]
- **Regular Maintenance:** Schedule regular property inspections and address maintenance issues promptly. Regularly maintained properties attract higher rents.

### *Managing for Greater Return on Investment*

To achieve the greatest return on your investment, you'll want to research and purchase properties that will generate the highest monthly profit. You'll also want properties that will allow you to maximize their potential and squeeze as much rent out of them. One way to do that is to find a single-family property, with the potential of adding a second unit. Duplexes and multifamily properties are also good choices for maximizing returns.

To see if a property will deliver a strong return on investment, you need to run the numbers. Always do the math for each potential property before you buy. I've included some calculations below. To complete them, you'll need the following numbers:

- **Purchase Price of the Property:** You can use either the listing price or the lowest offer you're willing to make on the property.
- **Additional Money for Repairs and Improvements:** Use the property tour and agent's input to assess any needed repairs or improvements. If you want to add a second unit to the property, calculate the estimated building costs.
- **Expected Monthly Rents:** Review other rental listings to see what a reasonable rent might be for your property. You can use Craigslist, Zillow, or Rentometer to get an idea of market rents for similar properties.
- **Anticipated Monthly Operating Costs:** Calculate the average monthly cost for property taxes, homeowner's insurance, routine maintenance, and any utilities not paid by the tenant. Maintenance costs could include HVAC service, landscaping, and gutter cleaning.

### *Example Annual Return on Investment Calculation*

To help you compare different investment properties, you can use this annual return on investment calculation. This calculation estimates how much profit an investment property could earn you as a percentage of the cost of that investment. A good return on investment for real estate is between 6 and 12 percent.[13] Use these formulas to calculate the annual return on investment as a percentage:

> *Total cash investment = purchase price + cost of repairs and improvements*
>
> *Annual return on investment = annual rental income - annual operating costs*
>
> *Percent annual return on investment = (annual return on investment ÷ total cash investment) X 100*

To demonstrate, let's say you're looking at a two-bedroom, two-bath single-family home with a $375,000 list price. You estimate investing another $25,000 in repairs and improvements.

Thus, for this example, the total cash investment would be:

> *$375,000 purchase price + $25,000 cost of repairs and improvements = $400,000 total cash investment*

Using this same example, you estimate your annual rental income to be $30,000. This annual rent amount is based on a review of Rentometer,[14] which projects you could charge $2,500 per month for rent. Twelve months multiplied by $2,500 is $30,000. Note, this example is not based on an actual Rentometer search.

You also estimate that your average monthly operating costs will be $750 per month. Twelve months multiplied by $750 is $9,000. So, your estimated average annual operating costs would be $9,000.

To calculate your annual return on investment in dollars, you subtract the annual operating costs from the annual rental income. Here's the annual return on investment formula:

*$30,000 annual rental income - $9,000 annual operating costs = $21,000 annual return on investment*

Next, to get the annual return on investment as a percentage, use this calculation:

*($21,000 annual return on investment ÷ $400,000 total cash investment) X 100 = 5.25 percent annual return on investment*

In this example, the estimated percent annual return on investment for this property is 5.25 percent. The next step would be to look at other properties for sale and use the same calculations to compare percent annual return on investment. Then choose the property with the highest percentage.

### B. Real Estate Investment Trusts

If you want to invest in real estate without the hassle of owning property, consider a real estate investment trust, also known as a REIT. A REIT is a trust company that owns and manages income-producing properties.

The trust sells shares of the REIT and pays out dividends to shareholders. REITs are required to distribute 90 percent of their taxable income as dividends.[15] Thus, many REITs regularly make solid dividend payouts, making them a great option for investors seeking steady income. You also have the option of reinvesting the dividends into additional shares.

There are a few types of REITs, but the ones I'm referring to here are called equity REITs. There are also mortgage REITs or mREITs, which is a company that invests in mortgages and mortgage-backed securities. These mREITs provide investors with mortgage interest income.

Similar to stocks, REITs are traded on major exchanges. You can purchase individual REITS or a collection of REITs packaged as a mutual fund or ETF fund.

REITs invest in commercial or residential real estate, including single-family homes, apartment buildings, hotels, medical facilities, retail spaces, and storage units. REITs can focus on a specific property type or hold multiple types of properties in their portfolios.

### *Managing Risk*

You can help manage your investment risk with REIT ETF index funds versus individual REITs. REIT ETF index funds would diversify your investments across multiple real estate companies. This diversification would help reduce your exposure to market volatility and provide you with a stable income.

REIT ETF index funds are also a low-cost investment option. This is because, like an index fund, REIT ETF index funds closely mirror an underlying REIT Index of publicly traded real estate companies. This makes managing these funds easier.

REIT ETF index fund shares are tradable on major stock exchanges, which also makes them much more liquid than owning individual real estate properties.

### *Example Annual Return on Investment Calculation*

The annual return on investment calculation for REIT ETFs includes the change in share price and the dividend payments to shareholders. Dividend payments are monthly or quarterly. This calculation is like the stock market annual return on investment calculation used earlier in this chapter.

You can calculate the annual return on investment for REIT ETFs by using the following formula:

> *Annual return on investment = (ending value + total dividend payments) - starting value*

Next, use this formula to get the percent annual return on investment:

> *Percent annual return on investment = (annual return on investment ÷ starting value) x 100*

For example, let's assume that at the beginning of 2024, you owned 2000 shares of iShares Core U.S. REIT ETF with stock symbol USRT. The share price was $54.10. Thus, your investment had a *starting value* of $108,200. At the end of

2024, the share price had increased to $57.30 per share. Therefore, your original 2000 shares have an *ending value* of $114,600. You also received quarterly dividend payments that totaled $3,200 for the year. Note, this example is not based on actual USRT results.

Using the USRT example, the annual return on investment calculation is:

*($114,600 ending value + $3,200 total dividend payments) - $108,200 starting value = $9,600 annual return on investment*

Next, to get the percent total annual return on investment, use this calculation:

*($9,600 annual return on investment ÷ $108,200 starting value) x 100 = 8.9 percent annual return on investment*

Based on these two calculations, your annual return on investment in USRT was $9,600 and your percent annual return on investment was 8.9.

### How to Implement a Solo Real Estate Investment Strategy

This section provides a step-by-step plan for implementing a solo real estate investment strategy. Whether you invest in a single-family home, duplex, or multifamily unit, this section will help you implement that strategy in three steps: 1) save up for the down payment or use equity from an existing home, 2) research properties for sale in your area, and 3) make a purchase offer.

### 1. Save Up for the Down Payment or Use Equity From an Existing Home

Decide on the type of rental property you want to buy. Review the average listing prices in your area. Then calculate how much you'll need to save for a 20 percent down payment.

If the median single-family home price is $400,000,[16] then you'll want to save at least $80,000. If it will take longer than five years to save the down payment, consider other investment options until you reach your down payment goal. For example, you could invest in stock market index funds or REIT ETFs.

Alternatively, if you own a home with enough equity, a loan officer or broker can help you explore a home equity loan or cash-out refinance. You could then use the equity loan or cash-out as the down payment for the rental property. Get qualified before you begin your search for properties.

### 2. Research Properties for Sale in Your Area

Once you have your down payment, it's time to look for a property to purchase.

Revisit the *Managing for Greater Return on Investment* and *Example Annual Return on Investment Calculation* sections earlier in this chapter.

For each potential property, calculate the annual return on investment. Besides the purchase price, determine if you'll need to invest in any repairs or improvements to get the property ready to rent. Research what you can expect to charge for rent, and calculate estimated operating costs.

For convenience, I've repeated the annual return on investment calculations below:

*Total cash investment = purchase price + cost of repairs and improvements*

*Annual return on investment = annual rental income - annual operating costs*

*Percent annual return on investment = (annual return on investment ÷ total cash investment) X 100*

You can also use the Investment Property Analysis Worksheet to assist you in gathering data and calculating the percent annual return on investment for each property. Use a separate worksheet for each property. Download and print copies of this worksheet at hermoneyrules.com/bonus.

After analyzing each potential property, compare their return on investment calculations and identify the ones with the highest percentage annual return on investment.

### 3. Make a Purchase Offer

Once you've identified properties with the best return on investment potential, make an offer on the one with the highest percentage annual return on investment. In case the owner rejects your offer or negotiations fail, you can then make an offer on the next best property.

Don't rush into this step. Keep looking for properties and researching them for the best potential return on investment. As you take time to find the best property, keep growing your down payment.

### How to Implement a REIT Investment Strategy

To invest in a REIT ETF index fund, follow the steps in the above section, *How to Implement Your Stock Investment Strategy.* Instead of choosing one of the recommended stock index funds listed in that section, you could invest in a REIT ETF index fund.

Based on my research, I've included below a selection of low-fee REIT ETF index funds recommended by financial experts. I suggest researching each of these, or others you find, before investing.

Recommended REIT ETF index funds:

SCHH Charles Schwab U.S. REIT ETF
Expense ratio 0.07 percent
Underlying index: Dow Jones Equity All REIT Capped

VNQ Vanguard Real Estate ETF
Expense ratio 0.13 percent
Underlying index: MSCI U.S. IMI/Real Estate 25-50

XLRE State Street The Real Estate Select Sector SPDR Fund
Expense ratio: 0.09 percent
Underlying index: S&P Real Estate Select Sector

USRT iShares Core U.S. REIT ETF
Expense ratio: 0.08 percent
Underlying index: FTSE Nareit / Equity REITs - INV

RWR SPDR Dow Jones REIT ETF
Expense ratio: 0.25 percent
Underlying index: Dow Jones U.S. Select REIT

## KEY POINTS

- Let your money work for you by investing in the stock market or real estate, the two best ways to build wealth.
- History shows that over time, the value of your investments will grow. There may be short-term ups and downs, but if you hold steady and take a long-term approach, your investments should grow exponentially.
- Research all potential investments and use annual return on investment calculations to help you choose the best ones.

## ACTION PLAN

In the companion *Her Money Rules! Financial Planner*, or your notebook, complete the following action steps:

- ☐ First, choose your overall investment strategy: invest in the stock market or invest in real estate. To help you choose, answer these questions: Which strategy are you most likely to fully implement and which strategy sounds the most fun? If you chose Option 1: Invest in the Stock Market as your overall investment strategy, complete the action plan steps below Option 1. If you choose Option 2: Invest in Real Estate, complete the action plan steps below Option 2.

Option 1: Invest in the Stock Market:

- ☐ Choose and write down your stock market investment strategy. If you are uncertain, reread this chapter. If you're still unsure, conduct additional research or consult with a financial advisor.
    - Option A: Index Funds
    - Option B: Non-Index Mutual Funds
    - Option C: Target Retirement Funds
    - Option D: Individual Stocks (not recommended)
- ☐ If you don't already have an investment or retirement account, decide on the type of account you want to open (*e.g. 401(k), Roth IRA, taxable investment account*). To help you decide, revisit the *How to Implement Your Stock Investment Strategy* section in this chapter. Then, choose which company to open your account with (*e.g. your employer's provider, Schwab, Fidelity, Vanguard*). Once you've chosen your provider, go to their website and follow the prompts to open your account.
- ☐ You have your investment account, and you've chosen your stock market investment strategy. Now, it's time to make an investment plan. Write your investment savings goal as a dollar amount and the date by when you'll reach your goal. Also, write how much you'll contribute to your investments each month. If you plan to invest right away, update your monthly budget to reflect that.

Option 2: Invest in Real Estate:

- ☐ Choose your real estate investment strategy: solo investing or REITs. If you choose solo investing, complete the action plan steps below the Solo Investing option. If you choose REITs, complete the action plan steps below the REITs option.

Solo Investing

- ☐ If choosing the solo investing option, you'll want to decide what type of property you want to invest in: single-family home, duplex, or multifamily home. Then research current property listings and analyze each property to determine the potential return on investment. During this analysis, calculate how much money you'll need to save and invest up front for each potential property. Do this by adding up the down payment and additional investments for repairs and improvements. You can download and print copies of the Investment Property Analysis worksheet at hermoneyrules.com/bonus. Use a separate worksheet for each property.
- ☐ Based on different property options and their expected price points, calculate how much money you'll need up front to fund your real estate investment. Then make a plan to save and grow that investment money. Also, update your budget to include your real estate investment savings.

REITs

- ☐ If you've chosen the REITs option, and you don't already have an investment or retirement account, decide on the type of account you want to open (e.g. *401(k), Roth IRA, taxable investment account*). To help you decide, revisit the *How to Implement Your Stock Investment Strategy* section in this chapter. Then, choose which company to open your account with (*e.g. your employer's provider, Schwab, Fidelity, Vanguard*). Once you've chosen your provider, go to their website and follow the prompts to open your account.
- ☐ Once you have your investment account, it's time to choose which REIT funds you'll invest in. There are REIT index funds, specialty REIT funds, and individual REIT investments. To help you decide, read the section *How to Implement a REIT Investment Strategy,* where I've listed recommended REIT ETF index funds. Please conduct additional research on your own before choosing which REIT funds to invest in.
- ☐ You have your investment account, and you've chosen which REIT funds to invest in. Now, it's time to make an investment plan. Write your investment savings goal as a dollar amount and a date by when you will reach your goal. Also, write how much you will contribute to your investments each month. If you plan to invest immediately, update your monthly budget to reflect that.

## COMING UP IN RULE 9: IMPLEMENT YOUR FINANCIAL PLAN AND TRACK YOUR PROGRESS

The next chapter focuses on the importance of taking consistent action toward reaching your big financial goal. You'll learn the steps to take each month to implement your One-Page Financial Plan and track your progress.

# RULE 9

# IMPLEMENT YOUR FINANCIAL PLAN AND TRACK YOUR PROGRESS

*"A goal without a plan is just a wish."*

*—Antoine de Saint-Exupéry*[1]

## ACTION PLAN

While I was writing this book, one of my clients, Kayla, shared her big financial goal with me. Kayla envisions building the kind of wealth that will allow her to live entirely off her investment income. With true financial freedom, she could leave her job behind and fully embrace her calling—creating art and sharing the beauty of the natural world.

Kayla and I worked together to create her One-Page Financial Plan for how she'll reach her big financial goal. Because, as Antoine de Saint-Exupéry said, "A goal without a plan is just a wish."

Having a plan is great, but perhaps Mr. de Saint-Exupéry's quote should've been—*A goal without a plan* [or action] *is just a wish.* Because what good is a goal or a plan without action? We must also implement our plan and take lots of consistent action.

For any goal, follow the Goal Achievement Cycle (Figure 1) to plan, implement, track, and revise your plan. Keep following this cycle until you reach your goal.

Figure 1. Goal Achievement Cycle

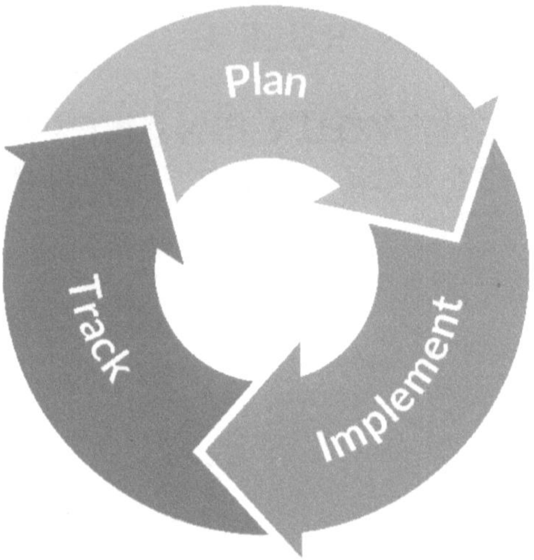


## READY, SET, GO!

If you haven't already, complete your One-Page Financial Plan using the companion *Her Money Rules! Financial Planner* or download the template at hermoneyrules.com/bonus.

Before implementing your plan, you'll need to craft your plan, and now is the time. Don't put this book on a shelf and forget about it. Take your path to wealth into your own hands. Complete your One-Page Financial Plan and begin implementing it this week. If you've already completed it, review it one more time and make any needed changes.

I promise if you create and implement your financial plan, you'll reach your big financial goals. Begin your journey to wealth and financial freedom now.

## IMPLEMENT YOUR PLAN

Once you've completed the companion *Her Money Rules! Financial Planner* and your One-Page Financial Plan, you've made a tremendous step. The next step is just as important—it's time for implementation.

Wouldn't it be amazing if we could simply write down our dreams, wish them into existence, and let the universe handle the rest? While I believe the universe supports us, offering a few miracles along the way, we still have to do our part. We need to show up, put in the effort, and take steps toward what we want. That's how the universe knows we're serious.

To ensure your success in implementing your plan, I recommend you take an hour each month to review and update your One-Page Financial Plan and track your progress. You can download and print additional copies of the One-Page Financial Plan template at hermoneyrules.com/bonus.

During the beginning of your scheduled time, take a few moments to reflect on the previous month. How did it go implementing your plan? What were your wins? What can you do differently in the upcoming month? Make sure you also review and update your:

- Big financial goal
- Spending plan
- SMART goals
- Action items

Identify the steps you need to take to reach your next milestone goal. Create new SMART goals, update your spending plan and monthly budget, and identify the action steps you'll take during the next month.

For the remaining time, complete the tracking worksheets as described in the action plan steps below.

## TRACK YOUR PROGRESS

Besides creating a plan and implementing your plan, you're more likely to reach your goals if you measure and track your progress.

There's a saying I heard often during my career as a government auditor—*what you measure gets done.* If you're measuring something, then you're more apt to act on the information. So, what you measure and track is what you'll focus on.

I've created tracking worksheets for you to review and update each month. These worksheets will help you track your progress and motivate you to put your One-Page Financial Plan into action. You can find the tracking worksheets in the companion *Her Money Rules! Financial Planner* or you can download them at hermoneyrules.com/bonus. The action plan steps at the end of this chapter will guide you in using these tracking worksheets.

## MEASURE AND TRACK YOUR NET WORTH

I've mentioned the concept of net worth throughout this book. It's like a financial scorecard—a snapshot of your overall financial health. Your net worth is the difference between your assets and your debts. Assets can include cash, investments, and property, while debts can include loans and credit card balances.

Your net worth can either be a positive or negative number. If you have more debt than assets, you'll have a negative net worth. In the Introduction, I shared that my net worth was negative $40,000 after attending graduate school. This was because I used student loans, credit cards, and all my savings and retirement investments to pay for tuition and living expenses.

Tracking your net worth is a helpful way to stay on course as you work toward your big financial goal. In fact, your big financial goal might even be a net worth goal. For example, if you're aiming to become a millionaire, your target net worth would be $1 million.

As you use a portion of your income to pay down debt, build your savings, or invest, your net worth will increase each month. Tracking your net worth doesn't just measure your financial strength; it can also encourage and motivate you as you watch that number grow.

Use the Quarterly Net Worth Tracking Worksheet to help you measure and track your net worth. You can find this worksheet in the companion *Her Money Rules! Financial Planner* or you can download it at hermoneyrules.com/bonus.

## KEY POINTS

- Besides creating your unique One-Page Financial Plan, you'll need to implement that plan to achieve your big financial goal.
- Consistent, devoted action is how we accomplish our goals.

- To set yourself up for success in implementing your plan, review and update your One-Page Financial Plan once a month.
- What you measure gets done, so it's also important to make time to track your progress each month.

## ACTION PLAN

Complete your One-Page Personal Financial Plan and the tracking worksheets described below, which can be found in the companion *Her Money Rules! Financial Planner.* You can also download and print additional copies of these worksheets at hermoneyrules.com/bonus.

- [ ] One-Page Personal Financial Plan template: Complete this template, then review and update it every month. Write your big financial goal at the top of your plan. Add your spending plan by assigning a percentage of your take-home pay to each spending category. Update and track your net worth quarterly. Then add your SMART goals and current and future action items.
- [ ] Monthly Goal Review Worksheet: Use this worksheet to track your monthly goal review. Include your big financial goal at the top of the worksheet.
- [ ] Monthly Habits Worksheet: Implement one new habit per month and commit to this habit on the Monthly Habits Worksheet.
- [ ] Monthly Expense Cutting Worksheet: Use this worksheet to review and track your monthly living expenses.

- ☐ Monthly Spending Tracking Worksheet: Use this worksheet to track and compare your actual spending totals and percentages each month.
- ☐ Monthly Income Tracking Worksheet: Use this worksheet to track your monthly income from each source. If you have only one job and one source of income, you can leave the other columns blank. As you create side hustles or assets to bring in additional income, you can add them to the additional columns.
- ☐ Monthly Emergency Fund Tracking Worksheet: Use this worksheet to track your progress toward reaching your emergency fund savings goal. Each month, record your savings deposits. If an emergency comes up, record any withdrawals.
- ☐ Monthly Debt Tracking Worksheet: If you have credit card or other consumer debt, use this monthly worksheet to record each debt payment.
- ☐ Monthly Investment Tracking Worksheet: Use this worksheet to record your monthly investment or savings transfers and any monthly earnings from interest, dividends, or changes in share value.
- ☐ Quarterly Net Worth Tracking Worksheet: Review this worksheet each month and update it each quarter. Use the worksheet to record and update the value of all your assets and debts. Then subtract your total debts from your total assets to calculate your net worth.

# CONCLUSION

*"Patience, persistence and perspiration make an unbeatable combination for success." —Napoleon Hill*[1]

## MONEY = FREEDOM

In the Introduction, I shared my journey to financial freedom, from struggles and frustrations to how real estate investing became the key to achieving my dreams.

When I was forty-two, I reached the point where I had enough money to have the freedom to quit my regular job. This year I turn fifty, so I've had eight years of freedom.

In those eight years, I've fulfilled my dream of traveling the world. My husband, Kent, and I have traveled an average of six months a year. Internationally, we've been to Europe three times, Mexico twice, and Thailand once. We've traveled across the northern U.S. in *Nugget*, our 20-foot camper van, and we plan to travel the southern route next year. We've traveled to Alaska via Canada and the Alaska Highway, also known as the Alcan Highway.

I've also been able to spend more quality time with family. This time has brought me closer to my daughters and sons. I became a grandmother three years ago, and it's been a blessing to have time to spend with my grandchild.

Writing this book has given me the chance to reflect on everything financial freedom has given me. It's an opportunity to thank my past self. I thank my twenty-three-year-old self for having the boldness to dream big and start this journey. I'm grateful to my thirty-three-year-old self for having the courage to invest in my first rental property. I appreciate my forty-two-year-old self for having the courage to quit my career and steady paycheck for a life of adventure and freedom.

Take immense action and implement what you've learned from this book. One day, your future self will thank you for your courage and dedication in working toward your big financial goal. Actually, thank yourself right now for dreaming big and embarking on this journey.

## GOAL + ACTION = RESULT

In Rule 2, I asked you to dream big and identify your big financial goal. This is a critical first step. But to accomplish your goal and believe it's possible, you also need to see yourself in the future having achieved that goal. Imagine yourself in the life you'll have. What is life like? How are you spending your time?

Once you have your goal, and you believe it's possible, the next step is to take action. You need to take consistent and committed action for as long as it takes.

If you've completed the action plan steps in each chapter, you now have your own One-Page Financial Plan. If you implement that plan, you will eventually reach your big financial goal. As Napoleon Hill suggests, have patience and persistence and you can succeed.

Trust the process, and keep taking action. As someone who has already made the journey, trust me when I say that time passes quickly. And time flies, whether or not you're working toward your dreams. Looking back, the past eight years of financial freedom have flown by. The prior eight years, the ones I spent taking action on my financial plan, flew by just as fast.

Again, imagine yourself reaching your big financial goal. Immerse yourself in that reality. Now tell yourself that the time to implement your plan to achieve that goal is totally worth it. Because it will be. And why not? Time will fly by whether or not you implement your plan. So why not implement your plan and honor the dreams of your current and future self?

## FINANCIAL FREEDOM IS NOW WITHIN YOUR REACH

In the Introduction, I promised that if you read this book and complete the action plan steps, you will gain:

- A clear and defined financial goal and a detailed plan to reach that goal.
- The right money mindset for being determined and unstoppable in reaching your big financial goal.
- The knowledge and action steps you need to cut expenses and increase your income.
- An investment strategy and plan to speed up your journey to wealth and financial freedom.

So, how did we do?

I hope you're feeling more empowered and in control of your financial destiny. You now understand that your financial beliefs and habits are a choice. You can change course, dream bigger, and follow the path to that dream—with lots of consistent action.

I also hope you now believe you deserve to achieve your big financial goal and that it's within your reach.

You have the tools and resources available to make your dreams come true and create the life you want to live. You are well on your way to financial wealth and freedom.

Remember: the journey won't always be easy. But don't give up when it gets hard. Be gritty and understand you can accomplish anything you set your mind to. You have a lot of action steps ahead of you, and you also have the universe on your side.

Keep planning. Keep taking action. Take the time to review and make adjustments to your plan. If you do, you'll go from being stuck with what you have now to having it *all*—whatever you can dream up.

## REVIEWING THE NINE MONEY RULES

Each of the nine money rules has helped launch your journey toward achieving your big financial goal and achieving financial freedom. Here's a summary of what you've learned:

### Rule 1. Transform How You Think About Money

- Gaining money skills and implementing money strategies are simple, but not easy.
- We limit what is possible in our lives by what we think is possible.
- Our money beliefs can either get in our way, or they can help us on our path to wealth and financial freedom.

- We make our worst decisions with our emotions. Instead, if we make money decisions and actions based on our goals and plans, we can logically and more effectively reach our goals.
- There are common money truths, and the sooner you understand them, the less likely you are to go down the wrong financial path.

## Rule 2. Get Clear on Your Big Financial Goal

- There are three steps to reaching any big goal: 1) Dream big, find your why, and name your big goal; 2) Believe your big goal is possible for you; and 3) Create a detailed plan and execute that plan with committed action.
- To achieve your big financial goal, it's important to believe strongly that you can achieve it.
- Clearly imagining your future self after reaching your big financial goal makes it easier to take action now.
- For your big financial goal and smaller milestone goals, use the SMART goal formula to ensure your goals are specific, measurable, achievable, realistic, and time-bound.

## Rule 3. Cut Your Biggest Expenses First

- We save money and build wealth only when our living expenses are less than our income.
- You can significantly reduce your living expenses by cutting your largest expenses, such as housing, transportation, healthcare, and food.

- Because housing is your biggest expense, it's important to find creative ways of reducing this expense, such as by downsizing or house hacking.
- Other ideas for saving money include cooking from scratch, rarely eating out, cutting subscriptions, reducing utility costs, and not buying things new. And being insured just enough—not over-insured or under-insured—and using self-insurance as much as you can.

## Rule 4. Create Your Perfect Budget

- Budgeting is a *must* for being mindful and thoughtful with our spending, living within our means, and reaching our big financial goals.
- Giving every dollar that comes your way a job and assigning it to a spending category will help you prioritize spending.
- The budget strategy of *using last month's paycheck for this month's bills* is critical for financial stability and ensures you only spend money you've already earned.
- The budget strategy of *paying yourself first* puts you in the habit of living within your means.

## Rule 5. Grow Your Income and Create Multiple Income Streams

- The more you maximize your current and lifetime income and invest that extra income, the quicker you'll reach your big financial goals.

- Becoming a lifelong learner and investing in your professional growth and development can help maximize your lifetime earnings.
- Increase your income further with multiple income streams, such as with passive income or other side hustle businesses.

## Rule 6. Build Your Emergency Fund

- Not having an emergency fund puts you at financial risk and unnecessary stress.
- Have an emergency fund with at least $500 and up to six months' worth of living expenses, depending on your unique financial situation.
- Use budgeting to save as much as you can until you reach your emergency fund goal.
- The quicker you reach your emergency savings goal, the sooner you'll have peace of mind and can tackle your other financial goals.

## Rule 7. Pay Off All Your Non-Mortgage Debt

- Accruing debt is a sign that we're spending more than we earn and living beyond our means.
- Debt gets in our way of achieving financial freedom because it becomes a monthly expense that won't go away until it's paid off.
- Strategies for paying off debt include paying off the highest interest debt first or paying off the smallest size debt first.

- Another strategy is to consolidate your debt to simplify your repayment and lower the interest rate.

### Rule 8. Choose Your Investment Strategy

- Let your money work for you by investing in the stock market or real estate, the two best ways to build wealth.
- History shows that over time, the value of your investments will grow. There may be short-term ups and downs, but if you hold steady and take a long-term approach, your investments should grow exponentially.
- Research all potential investments and use annual return on investment calculations to help you choose the best ones.

### Rule 9. Implement Your Financial Plan and Track Your Progress

- Besides creating your unique One-Page Financial Plan, you'll need to implement that plan to achieve your big financial goal.
- Consistent, devoted action is how we accomplish our goals.
- To set yourself up for success in implementing your plan, review and update your One-Page Financial Plan once a month.
- What you measure gets done, so it's also important to make time to track your progress each month.

## NEXT STEPS

You're now clear on the nine money rules for achieving your big financial goal. You've done the hard work to create your One-Page Financial Plan. Now, go forth and implement your plan. Be amazing. Create amazing.

I promise if you implement and follow through on your plan, you'll look back ten or twenty years from now and thank yourself. Because you'll have made it. You'll be living the lifestyle of your dreams and enjoying many perfect days.

I'd love to hear from you. Share your big financial goal with me! You can email me at shanda@hermoneyrules.com.

# ACKNOWLEDGMENTS

First, if it weren't for the many people who heard my story and encouraged me to write this book, it would probably still be on my to-do list. Thank you to all my friends and family who supported me in finishing this project. Kent, you have been my biggest fan as I pursue the art of writing books. Thank you for sharing my dream of becoming financially free so we could travel the world together! A big thanks to my parents, who shaped me to become an independent woman and who were the first to teach me about money. Thank you to my kids for listening to my endless advice on all things related to money and for not rolling your eyes too much. In all seriousness, I really wrote this book for you.

A special thank you to Amberly Grant, David Assid, and those who wish to remain anonymous. Your money stories helped shape the lessons in this book. I also want to thank Mary DeLateur and Erin LeVan for volunteering to be early readers and proofreaders of this book; your perceptive edits were essential in getting this book over the finish line.

# NOTES

## Introduction


1. Attributed to Warren Buffett extensively online.
2. Rachel F. Seidman, "Voices on Independence: Four Oral Histories About Building Women's Economic Power," *Smithsonian American Women's History Museum*, October 25, 2024, https://womenshistory.si.edu/blog/voices-independence-four-oral-histories-about-building-womens-economic-power.


## Rule 1


1. *The Dhammapada: A Collection of Verses; Being One of the Canonical Books of the Buddhists*, trans. and ed. F. Max Müller (Oxford: Clarendon Press, 1881), chap. 1, verse 1.
2. Ramsey Solutions, *The National Study of Millionaires*, accessed February 6, 2025, https://www.ramseysolutions.com/retirement/the-national-study-of-millionaires-research.
3. Lisa Ryan and Suzanne Dziurawiec, "Materialism and Its Relationship to Life Satisfaction," *Social Indicators Research* 55, no. 2 (2001): 185–197, accessed February 6, 2025, https://www.jstor.org/stable/27526951.

4. Amit Kumar, "The Unmatchable Brightness of Doing: Experiential Consumption Facilitates Greater Satisfaction than Spending on Material Possessions," *Current Opinion in Psychology* 46 (2022): 101343.
5. Robert T. Kiyosaki, *Rich Dad Poor Dad*, 2nd ed. (Scottsdale, AZ: Plata Publishing, 2017), 69-70.
6. Tim Campbell and Jordan Safane, "Average Stock Market Return: A Historical Perspective and Future Outlook," *Business Insider*, accessed February 6, 2025, https://www.businessinsider.com/personal-finance/investing/average-stock-market-return.
7. Dillon Jacobs, "Warren Buffett's Net Worth Over the Years," *FinMasters*, updated October 2, 2025, https://finmasters.com/warren-buffett-net-worth/.
8. Joe Dominguez and Vicki Robin, *Your Money or Your Life*, 3rd ed. (New York: Penguin Random House, 2022), chap. 8.

### Rule 2

1. Mary Oliver, "The Summer Day," in *New and Selected Poems* (Boston: Beacon Press, 1992), 94.
2. Peter Adeney, "About," *Mr. Money Mustache Blog*, accessed March 21, 2025, https://www.mrmoneymustache.com/about/; Peter Adeney, "The Arizona Experiment!," *Mr. Money Mustache Blog*, November 2, 2023, https://www.mrmoneymustache.com/2023/11/02/moving-to-culdesac/.
3. Peter Adeney, "Getting Rich: from Zero to Hero in One Blog Post," *Mr. Money Mustache Blog*, February 22, 2013, https://www.mrmoneymustache.com/2013/02/22/

getting-rich-from-zero-to-hero-in-one-blog-post/; Peter Adeney, "A Brief History of the 'Stash: How we Saved from Zero to Retirement in Nine Years," *Mr. Money Mustache Blog*, September 15, 2011, https://www.mrmoneymustache.com/2011/09/15/a-brief-history-of-the-stash-how-we-saved-from-zero-to-retirement-in-ten-years/.

4. Peter Adeney, "Getting Rich: from Zero to Hero in One Blog Post," *Mr. Money Mustache Blog*, February 22, 2013, https://www.mrmoneymustache.com/2013/02/22/getting-rich-from-zero-to-hero-in-one-blog-post/; Peter Adeney, "Mr. Money Mustache's Own Story," *Mr. Money Mustache Blog*, April 8, 2011, https://www.mrmoneymustache.com/2011/04/08/mr-money-mustaches-own-story/.
5. Gale Matthews, "The Impact of Commitment, Accountability, and Written Goals on Goal Achievement," faculty presentation, Department of Psychology, Dominican University of California, 2007.
6. Dana Anderson, "U.S. Home Prices Hit All-Time High," *Redfin News*, June 20, 2025, https://www.redfin.com/news/housing-market-update-home-sale-prices-hit-record-high/.
7. Charlie Munger, Berkshire Hathaway, "Annual Meeting," held May 3, 1999, Omaha, NE.
8. *Thoughts Become Things*. Directed by Mike Dooley. Windermere, FL: Tut's Adventurers Club, 2010. Streaming video.
9. Tony Robbins, Facebook page, accessed October 5, 2025, https://www.facebook.com/watch/?v=825861736353739.

10. Peter Adeney, "Getting Rich: from Zero to Hero in One Blog Post," *Mr. Money Mustache Blog*, February 22, 2013, https://www.mrmoneymustache.com/2013/02/22/getting-rich-from-zero-to-hero-in-one-blog-post/; Peter Adeney, "Mr. Money Mustache's Own Story," *Mr. Money Mustache Blog*, April 8, 2011, https://www.mrmoneymustache.com/2011/04/08/mr-money-mustaches-own-story/.
11. George T. Doran, "There's a S.M.A.R.T. Way to Write Management's Goals and Objectives," *Management Review* 70, no. 11 (November 1981): 35–36.

## Rule 3

1. Traditional Swedish proverb (attribution unverified).
2. Emmie Martin, "Suze Orman: If you waste money on coffee, it's like 'peeing $1 million down the drain,'" *CNBC.com*, March 28, 2019, https://www.cnbc.com/2019/03/28/suze-orman-spending-money-on-coffee-is-like-throwing-1-million-down-the-drain.html; "Stop Buying Lattes and Get Rich?," *The Become Wealth Blog*, accessed October 5, 2025, https://www.become.nz/articles/stop-buying-lattes.
3. Title CFR 24 Part 92.252 (2005); Jessica Blais, "How Much of Your Income Should Be Spent on Housing?," *NFCC Blog*, August 3, 2023, https://www.nfcc.org/blog/how-much-of-your-income-should-be-spent-on-housing/; Chris Clark, "'Deeply troubling': The 30% rule for housing costs is ignored by almost 8 in 10 Americans, study says — is it time to revisit this common budgeting technique?," *Moneywise*, updated August 27, 2024, https://moneywise.

com/real-estate/30-rule-for-housing-costs-is-ignored-by-almost-8-in-10-americans.

4. Mousumi Sarkar, *How American Homes Vary by the Year They Were Built*, Working Paper no. 2011-18, Housing and Household Economic Statistics, Demographic Directorate, U.S. Census Bureau, Washington, DC, June 2011.
5. Freddie Mac, *Primary Mortgage Market Survey®*, Week ending October 2, 2025, https://www.freddiemac.com/pmms.
6. For consumer guides and product reviews, see *Consumer Reports*, "Homepage," https://www.consumerreports.org.
7. IARC Working Group on the Evaluation of Carcinogenic Risks to Humans. *IARC Monographs on the Evaluation of Carcinogenic Risks to Humans*, no. 114. Lyon: International Agency for Research on Cancer, 2018.
8. Joel Fuhrman, *Eat for Life* (New York: HarperOne, 2011).
9. Alex Carver, "CarShield Cost." *MarketWatch Guides*, September 24, 2025, https://www.marketwatch.com/insurance-services/car-warranty/carshield-cost/; Carl Anthonoy, "How Much Does Endurance Warranty Coverage Cost?," *Automoblog*, June 16, 2025, https://www.automoblog.com/reviews/auto-warranty/endurance-cost/.
10. Ibid.
11. Adapted from Joshua Fields Millburn, "Everything Is 100% off If You Don't Buy It," *The Minimalists*, accessed October 5, 2025, https://www.theminimalists.com/dont/.
12. Peter Adeney, "Hypermiling: Expert driving to save 25% on gas." *Mr. Money Mustache Blog*, July 26, 2011, https://www.mrmoneymustache.com/2011/07/26/hypermiling-expert-driving-to-save-25-50-on-gas/.

## Rule 4

1. Attributed to Warren Buffett extensively online.
2. "Homepage," *YNAB*, https://www.ynab.com/.
3. Elizabeth Warren and Amelia Warren Tyagi, *All Your Worth: The Ultimate Lifetime Money Plan* (New York: Free Press, 2005).
4. Ron Blue, *Master Your Money: A Step-by-Step Plan for Experiencing Financial Contentment* (Chicago: Moody Publishers, 2004); Mitch Anthony, *The New Retirementality: Planning Your Life and Living Your Dreams...at Any Age You Want* (Hoboken, NJ: John Wiley & Sons, 2020).
5. "The Magic is in the Method," *YNAB*, accessed October 7, 2025, https://www.ynab.com/ynab-method.
6. George S. Clason, *The Richest Man in Babylon* (New York: Penguin Books, 2002; originally published 1926).
7. "Stretch Your Dollars—Without the Stress," *YNAB*, accessed October 7, 2025, https://www.ynab.com/blog/stretch-your-dollars-with-ynab.
8. "Homepage," *YNAB*, https://www.ynab.com/.
9. "EveryDollar Budget App," *Ramsey Solutions*, accessed October 7, 2025, https://store.ramseysolutions.com/money/tools-and-apps/everydollar-budget-app/.
10. "Homepage," *Goodbudget*, https://goodbudget.com/.
11. "Homepage," *Honeydue*, https://www.honeydue.com/.

## Rule 5


1. Jim Rohn, "You Can Have More—If You Become More," *Jim Rohn Blog*, January 7, 2018, https://www.jimrohn.com/become-more/.
2. Sheryl Sandberg, *Lean In: Women, Work, and the Will to Lead* (New York: Alfred A. Knopf, 2013).
3. "Homepage," *Thumbtack*, https://www.thumbtack.com/.
4. "Homepage," *Taskrabbit*, https://www.taskrabbit.com/.
5. Russell H. Conwell, *Acres of Diamonds* (New York: Penguin Books, 2020; originally published 1915).
6. "Homepage," *Side Hustle School*, https://sidehustleschool.com/.


## Rule 6


1. Frank Sonnenberg, *The Path to a Meaningful Life* (Seattle: Frank Sonnenberg, 2022)


## Rule 7


1. Emmie Martin, "Suze Orman: Pay off debt ASAP, and not because it costs you money," *CNBC Make It*, October 3, 2018, https://www.cnbc.com/2018/10/03/suze-orman-pay-off-debt-asap-and-not-because-it-costs-you-money.html.
2. Brian Beers, "Should I Pay Off Debt or Invest Extra Cash?," *Investopedia*, updated September 26, 2025, https://www.investopedia.com/articles/pf/08/invest-reduce-debt.asp; "Paying Down Debt vs. Investing," *Wells Fargo Advisors*,

accessed October 7, 2025, https://www.wellsfargoadvisors.com/planning/goals/paying-down-debt.htm.

3. Ibid.
4. Dave Ramsey, *The Total Money Makeover: A Proven Plan for Financial Fitness* (Nashville: Thomas Nelson, 2003).
5. "In Defense of the Home Mortgage: Not all Debt is Bad Debt," *Cogent Strategic Wealth*, accessed October 7, 2025, https://cogentsw.com/financial-planning/in-defense-of-the-home-mortgage-not-all-debt-is-bad-debt/; Jeff Ostrowski and Meaghan Hunt, "Should I pay off my mortgage or invest?," *Bankrate*, April 08, 2025, https://www.bankrate.com/mortgages/pay-off-mortgage-or-invest/.
6. Ali Hussain, "Economist Explains Why Buying a Home Isn't Always a Better Choice Than Renting," *Investopedia*, September 27, 2025, https://www.investopedia.com/economist-explains-why-buying-a-home-isn-t-always-a-better-choice-than-renting-11811486; Laura Beck, "Should You Rent or Buy Right Now? This Money Expert Says Only One Is the 'Superior Option,'" *Yahoo!finance*, September 30, 2025, https://finance.yahoo.com/news/rent-buy-now-money-expert-142145373.html; Marianne Garvey, "Finance Guru Slams Claims That Renting a Home Is a 'Waste of Money'—and Reveals How You Can Use It To Build Wealth," *realtor.com*, October 15, 2024, https://www.realtor.com/advice/rent/money-expert-ramit-sethi-renting-wealth/.
7. Rachel Cruze, "How to Pay Off Your Mortgage Early," *Ramsey Solutions*, March 21, 2025, https://www.ramseysolutions.com/real-estate/how-to-pay-off-mortgage-early; Jeff Ostrowski and Alice Holbrook, "Should I pay off my mortgage early?," *Bankrate*,

September 24, 2025, https://www.bankrate.com/mortgages/early-payoff/; Taylor Getler, "Should I Pay Off My Mortgage Early?," *NerdWallet*, March 31, 2025, https://www.nerdwallet.com/mortgages/learn/pay-off-mortgage.

8. "Homepage," Mortgage Calculator, https://www.mortgagecalculator.org/.

## Rule 8

1. Attributed to Margaret Bonanno extensively online.
2. James Royal, "What is the average stock market return?," *NerdWallet*, updated September 12, 2025, https://www.nerdwallet.com/article/investing/average-stock-market-return.
3. "Dow Jones - 100 Year Historical Chart," *Macrotrends*, accessed October 7, 2025, https://www.macrotrends.net/1319/dow-jones-100-year-historical-chart.
4. "S&P 500 - 100 Year Historical Chart," *Macrotrends*, accessed October 7, 2025, https://www.macrotrends.net/2324/sp-500-historical-chart-data; "Dow Jones - Historical Annual Returns (1914-2025)," *Macrotrends*, accessed October 7, 2025, https://www.macrotrends.net/2622/dow-jones-by-year-historical-annual-returns.
5. Robert Rich, "The Great Recession," *Federal Reserve History*, November 22, 2013, https://www.federalreservehistory.org/essays/great-recession-of-200709.
6. Ibid.
7. James Chen, "Market Milestones as the Bull Market Turns 10," *Investopedia*, updated October 16, 2019, https://www.investopedia.com/market-milestones-as-the-bull-market-turns-10-4588903.

8. Michael Santoli, "10 years ago this week, the market hit the climactic bottom of the Great Recession," *CNBC*, updated March 4, 2019, https://www.cnbc.com/2019/03/04/the-10th-anniversary-of-the-climactic-march-2009-market-bottom-arrives-this-week.html.
9. "News release: Vanguard Announces The Passing Of Founder John C. Bogle," The Vanguard Group, January 16, 2019, https://corporate.vanguard.com/content/corporatesite/us/en/corp/who-we-are/pressroom/Press-Release-Vanguard-Announces-Passing-Of-Founder-Jack-Bogle-011619.html.
10. Bryan Armour, "Measuring the Performance of Active Funds Against Their Passive Peers," *Morningstar*, April 2, 2025, https://www.morningstar.com/funds/measuring-performance-active-funds-against-their-passive-peers.
11. "Retirement topics - IRA contribution limits," *IRS*, updated September 22, 2025, https://www.irs.gov/retirement-plans/plan-participant-employee/retirement-topics-ira-contribution-limits.
12. Tia Politi, "The Move-out Process & Security Deposit Reconciliation" (webinar, Rental Owners Association - Lane County, October 19, 2023).
13. Jamie Johnson, "How to calculate return on rental property," *Rocket Mortgage*, September 17, 2025, https://www.rocketmortgage.com/learn/return-on-rental-property; "What Is a Good Cash on Cash Return?: A Complete Guide," *Mashvisor*, September 6, 2023, https://www.mashvisor.com/blog/cash-on-cash-return/.
14. To research rent estimates in your area, see Rentometer, "Homepage," https://www.rentometer.com/.

15. 26 U.S. Code § 857 (2025), https://uscode.house.gov/view.xhtml?req=(title:26%20section:857%20edition:prelim).
16. Dana Anderson, "U.S. Home Prices Hit All-Time High," Redfin News, June 20, 2025, https://www.redfin.com/news/housing-market-update-home-sale-prices-hit-record-high/.

## Rule 9

1. Attributed to Antoine de Saint-Exupéry, unverified origin.

## Conclusion

1. Napoleon Hill, *Think and Grow Rich* (Meriden, CT: The Ralston Society, 1937), 181.

## ALSO BY SHANDA K. MILLER

*"Shanda has made an important contribution to supervisors and their team members. She delivers her message in a very practical and understandable way."*
—Mary Henry Cameron, CPA, MBA, CFE

*"As an executive coach with 30 plus years of leadership experience, I am impressed with Shanda's teachings. She touches on the key knowledge any leader must have and uses the 'whole person' approach to learning and engaging and leading others."*
—Julie Pearson-Ruthven, HICC, Compass Consulting

# ABOUT THE AUTHOR

Shanda K. Miller is a bestselling author dedicated to helping others create their own version of an extraordinary life. From living in a school bus in her twenties to achieving financial freedom in her forties, Shanda has always sought to live life with intention and purpose.

Before quitting her job at forty-two to become location independent, Shanda worked in the fields of environmental science and government performance auditing. She has a bachelor's degree in environmental science from the University of Idaho and a master's degree in public administration from the University of Oregon.

Shanda spends half her time traveling the world. When not traveling, Shanda and her husband, Kent, live in Eugene, Oregon.

# HELP A FELLOW READER?

**Thank you for reading *Her Money Rules!***

I sincerely appreciate you investing your time to read this book. I hope you loved it!

To help other readers like you interested in achieving financial freedom, will you leave a review on Amazon?

Honestly, I would love to hear your thoughts and insights too. I welcome both positive and constructive feedback, as it helps me become a better writer and will help me improve the next version, as well as future books I release.

Please take two minutes now to leave a helpful review on Amazon.

Thank you so much!

- Shanda

www.ingramcontent.com/pod-product-compliance
Lightning Source LLC
LaVergne TN
LVHW100729061126
851857LV00011B/458
*9781733712804*